EXECUTIVE WOMEN GRIT

Powerful Stories of Women Who Earned the Silver Spoon

INTERVIEWS WITH CEO'S AND EXECUTIVES

Powerful Stories of Women Who Earned the Silver Spoon

Christine Gannon, CEO with Antoinette Farmer-Thompson, DHEd

ISBN: 978-1-7358719-0-5

For worldwide distribution. Printed in the U.S.A.

A Note from the Authors

Simultaneous to the research and publication of Constitutional Grit: Using Grit as the Catalyst for Female Equity in the C Suite, we interviewed high performing women across industry and sectors to better understand the path these women took to achieve success.

What follows are the stories of amazing female leaders who refused to allow any obstacles to stand in their way of achieving their dreams.

We hope you are as inspired as we are by their individual stories.

With admiration and appreciation,

Christine and Toni
Fall 2020

An Excerpt From

Constitutional Grit: Using Grit as the Catalyst for Female Equity in the C Suite (Amazon, 2020)

Simultaneous to determining the research approach, was the ever-increasing conversation around grit and its correlation with success. The foremost expert and leading psychologist, Dr. Angela Duckworth, captured our attention in an interview published in the Costco Connection magazine with a headline "Enthusiasm is common. Endurance is rare". You will recall the number of references to McKinsey earlier in the book regarding this complex conversation regarding disparities and dilemmas. Interestingly, early in Angela Duckworth's career, she worked as a management consultant for McKinsey & Company, however she left to pursue a career in teaching as a seventh-grade math teacher in a New York City public school. "Watching which students worked hard and did well and which students did not, taught her that sustained passion and effort [perseverance]-not intelligence or income-formed a cornerstone for future success." In her 2016 bestselling book, Grit: The Power of Passion and Perseverance, Duckworth outlines how grit is highly predictive of achievement throughout life. Her 2013 TED Talk on the subject has been watched by more than 14 million people and translated into 49 languages. During the TED Talk, Duckworth was uncertain whether grit could be built or taught. Since then, she and others, including

Eskereis-Winkler (another prominent psychologist focused on goal achievement), purport that grit can be cultivated. What if we were to develop grit in younger women and men, even those entering the workforce...Individual Grit that could lead to Executive Grit. If grit can be cultivated, could it conceivably become a central theme in a corporation's culture, helping companies encourage grit among their employees and therefore becoming grit-driven companies?

In editing the final copy of this book and winding down the research, Christine and her husband Dave were having a conversation about the different aspects of the book. Dave expressed his sincere appreciation for the overarching theme of executive female grit and his concern with aggregating individual, executive, corporate, and collective grit, instead of having a singular focus on individual grit. Christine explained the reasoning behind the larger scope by saying, "If we only captured a book about female executive grit and stories that are inspiring, it potentially ends there, another great, feel-good book that spotlights accomplished women and their road to success. By addressing the broader scope and challenging the corporate and collective entities, there is an opportunity to not only raise the roof around female executives who have made it to the C-Suite, but also to challenge the collective to make real change happen. There is a significant chance that those leaders and companies with grit, executive grit, will step up and address the gaps in their organizations. When they succeed and their senior leadership teams and boards look more inclusive and diverse, other organizations can and will follow in their footsteps. It becomes a powerful movement of inclusivity."

"Enthusiasm is common. Endurance is rare"

With the number of women reaching management levels and obtaining college degrees as well as advanced certifications, why are the number of women CEOs stagnating? Only 6.6 percent of Fortune 500 companies are run by female CEOs, causing Fortune to launch the 100X25 initiative, which is pushing for female CEOs to lead 100 of the Fortune 500 companies by 2025. Angela Duckworth states that, "Commonsense advice is one thing, but advice that is based on rigorous scientific research is better. I created the Grit Scale so that I could study grit as a scientist because you cannot study what you cannot measure."

"I realize," stated Margaret Perlis, "that the role of grit has become a 'topic du jour,' however, we seek to make it more than that...the true catalyst for change. Duckworth tweaked the definition to be 'perseverance and passion for long-term goals...context of exceptional performance and success'." When Christine was interviewing one of the women for this book, Angela Cody-Rouget, she was very passionate about grit and the role it played in her life. During the interview, she comments, "True grit does not happen overnight." Angela's story is compelling and one of many stories we captured that identifies the internal fortitude or grit that is required for success.

Deliberate practice of all things related to grit can be summarized by Theodore Roosevelt's "The Man in the Arena": The credit belongs to the [wo]man who is actually in the arena, whose face is marred by dust and sweat and blood; who strived valiantly; who errs, who comes again and again, because the is no effort without error and shortcoming.

Why Grit

Numerous studies have been conducted to determine the formula for achieving desired success, for determining who makes it and who does not. If there were an algorithm, would it entail intellect, inherent talent, skill, IQ, EQ, and to what degree? "While none of these factors have proven to generate any kind of miracle formula, research has found evidence that over any other measurable factor, possessing the quality of grit is the highest predictor of an individual achieving greatness". These are the auspices under which "The Rockefeller Foundation provided a grant for Korn Ferry, a top executive search firm, to design and execute a research project geared to developing action-oriented initiatives to create a sustainable pipeline of female CEOs". A similar approach was taken, and they were able to secure participation of 57 female CEOs, 41 from Fortune 1000 companies and 16 from privately held organizations. The research involved collecting "pivotal experiences either personal history and career progression, using Korn Ferry's executive online assessment to measure key personality traits and drivers that had an impact."

In a recent multi-faceted study, Advancing Women Leaders: Changing the Game for Women in the Workplace, the authors identify six competencies in the Linkage's Women Leadership Model. Centered around Competency One awareness are others such as bold, clear, connected, influential, and inspiring. Conversely, Sylvia Hewlett, a well-known expert in the area of talent innovation, wrote a book, Executive Presence: The Missing Link Between Merit and Success, wherein she states that "Executive presence (EP) is not a measure of performance: whether, indeed, you hit the numbers, attain the ratings, or actually have a transformative idea. Rather it is a measure of image: whether you signal to others that you have what it takes, that you're star material." Her Center for Talent Innovation launched a study to crack the EP code. Surveys were sent to more than 4,000 college educated professionals, of which 268 were senior executives. Congruently, 40 focus groups and leader interviews were conducted. Their finding was that "EP rests on three pillars: How you act (gravitas), How you speak (communication), and How you look (appearance)".

At the Core

If we take a look at human beings in general, regardless of gender, we find there are five core character traits from which all personalities stem, called The Big Five. They are: Openness, Conscientiousness, Extroversion, Agreeableness, and Neurotic. Each exists on a continuum with its opposite on the other end, and our personality is the expression of the dynamic interaction of each and all at any given time. One minute, a person may feel more agreeable, the next more neurotic, but fortunately, day-to-day, most of us collectively remain fairly stable. Whew, is that ever a relief!

According to Duckworth, conscientiousness is the character trait most closely associated with grit. However, it seems that there are two types, and a leader's level of success will depend on which type they possess. Conscientiousness in this context means careful and painstakingly meticulous. The achievement-oriented individual is one who works tirelessly, tries to do a good job, and completes the task at hand, whereas the dependable person is more notably self-controlled and conventional. This encompasses much of the leadership landscape. Not surprisingly, achievement-orientated traits predict job proficiency and educational success far better than dependability. A self-controlled person who never steps out of line may fail to reach the same heights as their more mercurial friends. In other words, in the context of conscientious, grit, and success, it is important to commit to "go for the gold" rather than just show up for practice.

Christine interviewed Pam Gaber of Gabriel's Angels, and along with a very compelling story, she shared her thoughts about grit: "I read Angela Duckworth's book when it first came out after I read a review about it. The book resonated with me as I said to myself, 'This is it! It is the term for persevering in the face of adversity and never giving up.' To me, grit is the one term that embraces all that makes one successful, such as creating a village of support, having kick-ass resilience, and being willing to change your course of direction for the greater good."

Resilience: Optimism, Confidence, and Creativity

Resilience. Within the female population, female veterans are a group that demonstrate incredible resilience with courage, optimism, creativity, and most certainly confidence. Female veterans comprise

17 percent of the post-9/11 veteran population and are the fastest-growing sub-population of the veteran community, according to data from the Institute for Veterans and Military Families (IVMF). These women are also increasingly starting and growing businesses, even in the previously male-dominated STEM (science, technology, engineer, mathematics) fields. In fact, female veterans are twice as likely to pursue STEM-related occupations as are their civilian counterparts. The research shows that high-performing entrepreneurs tend to demonstrate solid decision-making and high levels of confidence, independence and high self-efficacy–even within chaotic environments. Considering their military service background and exposure to multiple, often dangerous, environments, female veterans are well known to possess these skills. Still, female entrepreneurs encounter challenges. In an IVMF/Syracuse University study, over 83 percent of female veterans surveyed cited obstacles in starting their own businesses. For female veterans and female professionals alike, resilience keeps women optimistic, confident, and creative in situations that create challenge.

Even with more women than ever stepping into roles with higher levels of responsibility or starting their own companies, it is still a stark reality in this leadership landscape that once a woman reaches the highest levels in a company or organization, she will likely have no other female counterparts at the same level.

From 2012 - 2020, IBM had a phenomenal female CEO, Ginny Rometty, leading the charge. Christine's career at IBM finished prior to Ms. Rometty's CEO assignment, but she was fortunate to have several female executives in her circle who were amazing trailblazers who paved the way for other women in the organization. In 2007, after leaving a highly successful career as a Transformation Executive at IBM, Christine became an entrepreneur and the CEO of Brightworks Consulting. With multi-level corporate experience and a host of executive consultants on contract, Brightworks began as an executive coaching and recruiting firm, and has expanded several times over the years to accommodate for industry demand and change. Today, Brightworks Consulting successfully serves the public and private sector with strategic planning, community outreach/engagement initiatives, and general management consulting. Christine notes, "As a female CEO, it's absolutely imperative to have resilience, optimism, courage and people who believe in you. Whether it is the CEO of a company you do business with, a potential business partner, staff working for your company, or an influencer in a key industry, people want to believe in you and your mission. Do they understand what your capabilities and talents are? They are relying on you as the CEO to tell them what you can do for them. For women to succeed as CEOs, courage, optimism, and resilience make the absolute difference between successfully running a company or becoming a statistic."

Recognizing the unique challenges and opportunities women face as they rise through the leadership ranks in public, private, and non-profit organizations both domestically and on a global scale, Brightworks Consulting launched the Women in Leadership Institute™ in 2018. Integrating the art of leadership with professional and personal development strategies to help women at all levels of their career, the Institute leverages the success of women where they are today, integrating new content focused on enhancing their business acumen, leadership skills, and corporate climate astuteness. With the publishing of this book, the Institute will expand its reach to men and women running organizations who want to solve the gender disparity in their own companies. Notes Christine, "With U.S.-based companies employing over half of the domestic female population, we know we must do better to provide a roadmap for women and men to resolve gender equity in the C-Suite."

McKinsey's recent Women in the Workplace 2019 report found that absence of female representation can often carry negative effects. In this study, McKinsey highlights that "when there's just one woman at the C-suite table, women were 49 percent more likely to have their judgment questioned than men (32 percent), and to be mistaken for a junior employee (35 percent vs. 15 percent)." Resilience is often demanded in this type of environment for women. In addition to that staggering fact, "Women are far more likely than men (24 percent vs. 14 percent) to suffer unprofessional comments and remarks when they are the only female in the room."

Have we made any notable progress?

Excellence vs. Perfection

Did you know that most women who possess immense amounts of grit refuse to get on the perfection train and instead dig deeper into their grit reserves? They strive for excellence! Do you know what the difference is? Perfection could be related to excellence, but not really. You will see that perfection shows up at the most inopportune times, raising the anxiety of everyone around the person who is striving for it. It could involve a big presentation, a family photo shoot with little ones, meeting a prospective client, or trying to close a deal. What does it look like? Tense energy swirling around the person who has expectations that most often cannot be met. The expectation of themselves and those around them are off the chart and unachievable, but they are determined to try as if they were not. We are in no way discounting that there are times when perfection is necessary to establish certain rules and standards. For example, the on our next airplane flight, we will be eternally grateful the maintenance crew made sure everything was in perfect working order and the gas tanks were full. We are not talking about those kinds of situations, though. Perfection, "a perception of an ideal, and pursuing it is like chasing a hallucination. Anxiety, low self-esteem, obsessive compulsive disorder, substance abuse, and clinical depression are only a few of the conditions ascribed to perfectionism…and to be clear, those are ominous barriers to success."

Margaret Perlis of Forbes writes, "Excellence is an attitude, not an endgame. The word excellence is derived from the Greek word Arête which is bound with the notion of fulfillment of purpose or function and is closely associated with virtue. It is far more forgiving, allowing and embracing failure and vulnerability on the ongoing quest for improvement. It allows for disappointment and prioritizes progress over perfection. Like excellence, grit is an attitude about, to paraphrase Tennyson…seeking, striving, finding, and never yielding."

Defining Grit / Characteristics of Grit/ Overview/Individual Grit

Tenacity, resolve, persistence, drive, and relentless determination. All these words or phrases describe grit, and most people possess it. The technical definition of grit is "a personality trait possessed by individuals who demonstrate passion and perseverance toward a goal despite being confronted by significant obstacles and distractions. Those who possess grit are able to self-regulate and postpone their need for positive reinforcement while working diligently on a task." Filled with passion and a thirst for achieving goals, women with an awareness of their own grit rise up with renewed strength and purpose, and are resolute when they have suffered failure, a setback, or a time when things just didn't turn out the way they were supposed to. Women with grit are passionate, persistent, and filled with a sense of knowing they will find a way, even when there seemingly is not a way. What if the path could be illuminated? What if there were a formula or algorithm that would allow women to achieve C-level positions more rapidly?

According to Angela Duckworth, it is not innate intelligence but resolve and tenacity that create success. In other words, grit. Defined, grit is a psychological marker that identifies having a passion for the long game and remaining perseverant to achieve the final inning. It is the resilience to go on with renewed purpose. It is the commitment to your goals and a belief in yourself and/or to a greater cause. The beauty of grit is that it's not just a popular buzzword – it's a powerful and formidable motivational tool that can be used in both work and personal life.

Where does grit come into the picture for most women?

The women we've interviewed prove that it's not feelings of worth, insecurities, or one's title that helps her achieve the dream. It's GRIT. It's the persistence and strong-willed perseverance that has enabled women throughout history to achieve their dreams and goals.

Women grow grit in many ways, but two were significantly evident in our research. Women often grow grit from the core of who they are, through what they've experienced, and by having a solid purpose. They also cultivate it from choosing a tribe of other women who have grit and/or surrounding themselves with both genders who are either grittier than or as gritty as they are. It's no secret that who we surround ourselves with has the ability to shape our thinking, our identity, and our lives. Proverbs 13:20 says, "Walk with the wise and become wise, for a companion of fools suffers harm." When we choose to be a part of a culture and engage in community that can and does overcome adversity, we develop grit and learn that even when the odds seem impossible, we can overcome.

In our research, we found several studies conducted with all different types of populations and age groups. One study focused on high school seniors. The researcher followed over 100 students, beginning their senior year in high school, and continued for the next 60 months. Three characteristics stood out in terms of their success quotient: academic prowess, leadership, and follow-through. Out of the three, follow-through was the most important aspect of the success any of them achieved. To stick with a project, even when obstacles seem insurmountable, and to overcome challenges takes grit. Whether they started their life post-high school with or without grit, the study concluded that following through was the key ingredient. Without it, few found success.

Individual Grit is defined as having the courage and confidence to show the strength of your character. Executive Grit, on the other hand, often means "finding perseverance and sustainable passion to work toward long-term goals, rather than growing discouraged and giving up when things do not work out as quickly as one might hope." Regardless of how the term is categorized (individual or executive), we know that grit is the solution to ensuring women and men are equipped to move the needle towards inclusivity and gender parity.

Research has shown that neither gender bias training nor a heightened awareness of gender equality is having an effect on changing organizational behavior. By having the necessary grit to work through the differences both men and women bring to the office and implementing models and algorithms that will change behavior, organizations will be able to recognize the benefit of having equal representation of men and women in the C-Suite.

Yes, grit is a motivational subject, often undervalued in its importance in our future and past. This chapter is intended to serve as a reminder of all our historical victories as well as our future battles, both of which should elevate our level of endurance and drive towards excellence – as individuals, organizations, and communities. Remember, you yourself have slayed dragons, climbed what others might consider unconquerable mountains, and cracked, even broken your own glass ceilings.

If Duckworth found grit to be the greatest predictor of success for children conquering math, then can it not also be a predictor of those who will accelerate the advancement of your organization? Executives, both male and female, make selections that indicate a lack of understanding of the importance of creating a workforce of warriors. What happens when you put a bunch of grit-driven folks together? What can be accomplished? If you are to build the best possible team, be sure to distinguish those that are gritty from those that are greedy, and those that are relentless from those that are reckless. Making a grit assessment of yourself and others can help to drive exponential results, both personal and organizational.

Continuing with the considerations of possessing Executive Grit, the authors not only consulted the writings and hypothesis of Angela Duckworth but decided to interview women executives to understand more deeply what differentiates grit from Executive Grit (from our perspective) and how these women made the transformation.

"You gain strength, courage and confidence by every experience in which you really stop to look fear in the face. You are able to say to yourself, I have lived through this horror. I can take the next thing that comes along. You must do the thing you think you cannot do.'"

—Eleanor Roosevelt

EXECUTIVE GRIT MODEL

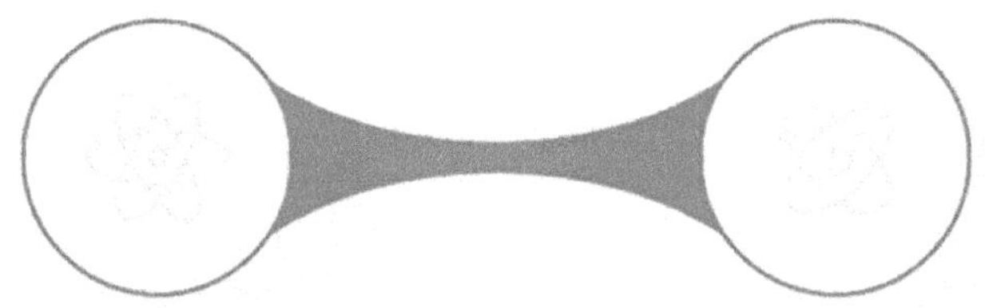

ANGELA DUCKWORTH GRIT SCALE	EXECUTIVE GRIT MODEL
New ideas and projects sometimes **distract** me from previous ones.	**Executive focus and single mindedness** ○ Cognitive Control ○ Personalized employee engagement
Setbacks don't discourage me. **Idon't give up** easily. Setbacks don't discourage me. Idon't give up easily.	**Executive failure and reflective practice** ○ Failure resume ○ Reflection – a conscious form of practice
I often set a goal but later choose to pursue a different one.	**Executive approach to goal setting** ○ Symphonic goal setting ○ Cross-disciplinary planning and operations
I am a hard worker I have difficulty **maintaining my focus** on projects that take more **than a few months** to complete.	**How executives work** ○ Executive productivity – time management and operational pulse points ○ Executive leaders measure their success
My interests change from year to year. I am diligent. I never give up.	Executive Functioning 4 core behaviors – decision making, impactful engagement, proactivity, reliability
I have been obsessed with a certain idea or project for a short time but later lost interest.	Do CEOs obsess, and if so, how is it manifested? Obsessions become opportunities.
	The Female Factor – Assessment an the organizational leadership landscape

The authors developed their own Executive Grit Model © as shown beside Angela Duckworth's model of the Grit Scale

EXECUTIVE WOMEN GRIT

Chief Jeri Williams

City of Phoenix Police Department

Best childhood memories.

Chief Williams brightens as she recalls times at the amusement parks such as Six Flags and Busch Gardens with her Uncle Bill. After her parents divorced, this would be one of the highlights of the summer where her uncle would want to "expose us to things." This would be an outing with him and up to ten children at a time, all of whom were under the age of 16.

Favorite games to play growing up and do any of those relate to who you are or what you do today.

Ivy, an older cheerleader, would teach cheers to the younger girls in the neighborhood, and Jeri remembers being inspired to the point where she would then spend the rest of the time primarily singing and entertaining. Her greatest performances included songs from the Emotions, Supremes, and Temptations. This may have led to her love for theater and the motivation for studying theatre as a college student.

From the movie Fallen, can you define what moment this was for you?

There was an opening in Oxnard, California for the Chief of Police. The initial interview went well, however, "It is not likely that they will give me this job," she thought to herself. However, with the interview and a written exercise, even an exam, Jeri was ranked the #1 candidate. Final interviews were on a Thursday, and she was told they would narrow the field to the top three candidates. If selected, final interviews would be held the upcoming Monday with the City Manager. Only at that point did she say to herself, "I could actually get this job." Perhaps this confirmation came from a recent sermon preached by Pastor Benjamin Thomas, Sr.: "If you want to walk on water, you have to get out of the boat." Following Monday's interview, she was offered the Oxnard Chief of Police position which required an immediate decision and transition. Her choice to take the job was her Fallen Moment. She did not expect to get the job, perhaps not wanting to face the most dramatic change this would cause in her life…the fact that she would live alone for the first time in her life. Of course, there was the leaving behind of all that was comfortable – knowledge in her current role, teenage boys, and her husband. Despite these significant unknowns, she said yes to Oxnard.

What jobs or experiences contributed the most to your success? Why?

As a Maryvale high school graduate, Chief Williams grew up in what was considered a middle-class neighborhood in the 1980s.

She was accepted to Texas Tech, but failed out of school her first semester. After evaluating her options, she would find her way to Arizona State University and earn a degree in Fine Arts. Her goal at that time was to get a job with Pan Am Airlines, however, was told she was "too chubby." That led to the best decision ever made – going into law enforcement where she was not only accepted for who she was but was a welcomed change as a female officer.

If your career could be told in a story, what would be the conflict, climax, and the antagonist, and what do you project to be a happy ending?

As an officer, Chief Williams began to standout in every position – patrol, bicycle unit, detective, P&P, recruitment, Commander, then Assistant Chief. She went on to Oxnard where she became police chief for five years.

What did you do differently from colleagues to get to where you are?

A perfect blend of friend, supervisor, leader. Someone who gives everyone and anyone the same attention and respect. Her colleagues agreed. Chief Williams is said to have a way of making everyone feel special, experiencing an extraordinary connection. Resultantly, people are more relaxed and offer the best ideas and thus their best selves. When seeing the uniform, there of course is admiration of the position, but also assumptions that "I will act a certain way." She proudly states her age: "I am 52 years old" and says she will never forget from whence she has come. This is what makes Chief Williams approachable. From that conversation, it was clear that others are more formal in their interactions, however the Chief wants to create personal connections whenever and wherever she can.

Who or what has been your greatest inspiration?

Chief Williams immediately states, "My mom was my greatest inspiration," never having compromised on "us, her children." We were taught to never forget where we are from. Perhaps that is why she is deemed so approachable by her colleagues, even in a position of power.

What does grit mean to you?

"It means refusing to fail. I have never had permission to fail."

Which characteristics do you possess the most of and the least of?

Courage – One of the most courageous acts of a leader is to protect their team. The police department, especially in today's ethos, finds itself in a constant state of explaining and defending not only their actions but their honor. Having said that, Chief Williams describes an incident where her team did exactly what was expected but was still criticized by the community when unwarranted. However, the team did not waver, suffer, or lose faith. Excellence vs. Perfection – Chief Williams is not a perfectionist and does not require that of others. However, she does expect everyone to do their best. "When meeting me for the first time and I'm tired, that would not be acceptable. I owe it to you to be my best self."

Grittiest moments to date.

As a leader, you have to be unwilling to compromise your morals, values, and beliefs. I have had several instances where "I felt as though I could bend, it was uncomfortable, I don't know that I would still be here had I done so." It is important to remain especially confident in the midst of trials, which requires quite a few walks with the dog, Jermaine. The most memorable incident was being head of the precinct when receiving a call from her former supervisor, Assistant Chief Jack. There was an incident involving a Council Member. Councilman Mike Johnson, at 4:22AM, had an exchange with an officer who ultimately reported to then Commander William's team, an incident that could get her boss fired. She described the time the phone rang at 4:22AM. On the other end was Councilman Michael Johnson. A well-publicized "incident where Councilman Johnson was handcuffed and thrown to the ground by a Phoenix police officer –an officer whom the Phoenix Police Department refused to identify – as the councilman was trying to assist a neighbor whose house was on fire." She stood up for her officer even then. To her surprise, this would lead to an opportunity of a lifetime: an expanded position to include community engagement and SWAT. No doubt, this deepened experience and the ability to completely turn the situation around using an innovative approach to community policing was the very expertise that assisted in securing the Chief of Oxnard position.

Mentorship vs. Sponsorship –what is the difference?

Sponsorship is what is done to promote someone you know, a "good kid," perhaps for whom you make a call of support. Sponsorship requires some level of commitment but not a great deal of time. As Assistant Chief, "I had a few notable mentors, the first of whom was a female, Commander Marsha Forient, who was definitely instrumental in charting my course." Others included Jack Harris, Mike Frazier, and Alton Washington.

What are some words of wisdom and no-nonsense advice you have received?

Luke 12:48 – "To whom much is given, much is required." Also, "continue to be yourself because you are enough." I am now remembering Chief Williams' ministerial ordination, which takes years and commitment to complete. She was always well prepared and insightful.

Words of nonsense would still be those that came from Pan Am Airlines, "who told me I was too chubby/husky to become a flight attendant." However, there is true gratefulness for the rejection, as it allowed her to find her true passion and path.

What is the greatest difference between you and your male counterpart, if any?

Chief Williams answered this question the way a number of women would. "Most male counterparts had the benefit of having a wife. Like most moms, I had to deal with Pop Warner practice, studying for the lieutenant exam, being the community wife, making dinner, picking up kids, raising kids, and ensuring there was a hot meal before and after school. However, we made it work."

If you had to do something all over again, good or bad, what would it be?

Out of all the responses she could have given, Chief Williams said, "I should have learned Spanish." Having taken Spanish throughout her high school and college careers, she wishes for greater fluency. Looking back longingly is not something the Chief does. She stated, "We make it work; you become a pro, and you are able to do so and always keep lipstick in your pocket."

If we are to make strides towards Fortune's goal of 100X25, we must:

Improvements and strides have been made. There are five black female chiefs in some of the largest cities in America – Phoenix, Dallas, Portland, Raleigh, and Pittsburgh.

Is this possible in your industry...why?

Yes, there are a number of opportunities. For example, the last five chief recruitment advertisements stated that they were "looking for women." This would require, more than anything, 24-hour childcare and transportation. How do you do this without a safe place to put your kids? There is a need for an "all-inclusive service, which would allow women a safe place for their children." Chief Williams mentions her gratefulness to Miss Fischer, who was that haven for her children.

Essential daily or weekly reads:

The Bible, sometimes twice a day. Others around her have learned to use scripture to assist in helping her find the "reset button." Proverbs 3:4-5 "Trust in the LORD with all your heart and lean not on your own understanding; in all your ways submit to Him, and He will make your paths straight."

Favorite movie of all times and why?

"The Color Purple" – "I still cry at the end." It speaks of the resiliency of the human spirit; anyone could be Celie. Chief Williams' second favorite movie is "Friday." She has learned to adopt the philosophy and phrase, "Bye Felicia". Next might be "The Help" and "The Shack." She remembers reading these on the plane.

When I am not working, I am:

A chef who specializes in tacos, rice, beans, and peach cobbler.

It is essential for women to know _____ and do _____:

It is important to self-affirm every day that who you are is okay.

When I was at a low point, even my lowest point, it was important that I do _____to survive:

Pray.

If I could redo/relive a professional moment, it would be:

The day/night of the Mike Johnson incident. I never walked over to get involved with the employee. "I regret that part of the day, the incident."

When equating my life and success to a real person or fictitious character, I would choose:

Wonder Woman, Linda Carter: "She was bad, pretty, and fine."

People would be surprised if they knew I...

I was a cheerleader and afraid of heights.

Jenny Poon, Founder
CO+HOOTS

Best childhood memories.

Growing up in Minnesota in her parent's restaurant at six years old, playing in the basement in the storage room (very tiny). My older brother and sister using kitchen supplies napkins, bags of rice, cans of tomato, all of which we would use to come up with random games for entertainment, mostly designed by my brother whom I admire. Jumping around in a room playing tag – cutting carrots, making up little games. They were not allowed to take toys into the restaurant and her brother was the master of jumping on things and pretending the floor was lava. All this activity would of course lead to exhaustion and eventually sleep.

Favorite games to play growing up? Do any of those relate to who you are or what you do today?

Different board games, making own version of Monopoly related to US cities. Knights or Dragons, own board, own rules. I started participating, coming up with games together. Then, on to creating motion videos from an old school camcorder used to record for one second, transforming to motion videos by her brother.

From the movie "Fallen," can you define what moment this was for you?

Jenny's Fallen experience comes through that of her mother who came from Vietnam on a boat for 30 days. The boat was out of gas and out of food. "Being on the boat with all of those men… anywhere was better than where Mom was." Viewing her mother's experience as a great adventure, "I knew I could make it…I think about it a lot. How can I help others who have their own families, living middle class and above?" In 2012, in Dinkytown the restaurant was being bulldozed to make room for apartment complexes. Although the restaurant was there for 35 years, no consideration given, as someone wanted to purchase it. There was backlash, a lot of fearmongering. The neighborhood had become gentrified and her family was told, "You are going to have to leave one way or another." Other small businesses took a buyout, but her family had another 6- to 7-year lease. Close to retirement and not having enough to sustain the family's livelihood, her family decided to close. This became a big news story as everyone learned that the developer was shady. Hence the racist article written stating there is "no reason this business should hold up development as it should go to Americans so they can prosper." Being distant, I could see this caused a visceral reaction; knowing they had no understanding of what their parents had endured. They have been here for over 40 years, no government subsidies, built and put kids through college, and helped their community grow. Diversity should be something to celebrate especially given the adversity refugees endure.

Your educational and work experience – what jobs or experiences contributed the most to your success and why?

Born in Minnesota, Jenny went to public school then University of Minnesota. Because of dual enrollment, she was able to complete the first two years of college while in high school. Jenny's academic interest included journalism, advertising, and global studies. She taught English in China, did an internship and became a graphic designer and journalist. After graduating, she joined a publication company when it shut down, but came to Arizona (with husband) as an Art Director for Arizona Republic. The recession hit, laying off 50% of staff which launched her into entrepreneurial efforts. This is when she took a lot of freelance work, extra work, whatever was required to make money and survive. Working hard came easy especially watching her parents and she did not see it as being a workaholic, just taking on more work. Things began to improve. What should she do next? She launched a business with a number of clients, which was enough to sustain and keep them afloat. The work began to pick up and she had to hire. She then realized the asset of having a physical office space which could be not only affordable for others but also inspirational.

If your career could be told in a story, what would be the conflict, climax, the antagonist and what do you project to be a happy ending?

"A bunch of people??? make it, but it will break you." Every few years, "This is it." Little stories with the overarching theme, "If you do not make, you will break." Every few years there would be a new vision/ new business but ending in a stolen business model.

What did you do differently from colleagues to get to where you are?

Jenny considers herself "genuinely a great collaborator." She does not take no for an answer and will find a way for people to say yes. She often tells potential clients, "There will be a point for us to work together." She realized the value of being patient in the process.

Who or what has been your greatest inspiration?

Jenny's mom has been her greatest inspiration. When considering all that she has been through and figured out how to build businesses with no huge investors. Before loans were given to women, she worked out deals with owners and every month paid them back. She certainly had to be creative and innovative...building and withstanding would be the themes of her life.

Which characteristics do you possess most?

Excellence vs. Perfection. She admits that she "has incredibly high expectations." Working on concepts with different teams can be challenging. There is sometimes no straight path, similar to the U.S. founders and their process, however remembering there is no one way, one must trust the process and know others will arrive at the same place, perhaps a while after you.

Resilience. Reframing challenges is something she experienced/observed firsthand when her mom's store burned down, and they had to start over. Therefore when "I see problems and challenges, I am quick to figure out a solution, knowing the high I will feel once solved."

Stories of female grit...your grittiest moments to date?

Jenny started a non-profit four years ago, Cohoots, rooted in giving back. If a person or organization has a particular skill, she saw value in having them share their skills, creating an enterprise of diverse entrepreneurs. Initially, there were a great deal of middle-class white males who were wealthier. Jenny had a vision of expanding the opportunity while strengthening the population at the same time. She saved money for four years, but the foundation was expanded when a mutual friend came on board. They got along fine. Given that Jenny had thrown all her savings in, it was disappointing to find the partner could not make a go of it although she had been given a year's runway to make it sustainable. Jenny admits, "I over course-corrected and assumed she would get there without making her accountable." Nine months later the bank account was depleted, and the company was riddled with misspending and miscommunication. Now, she has found middle ground. She started over by raising additional funds, and implemented systems to track progress, making sure the impact is really there. It is important to make sure you are partnered with people with similar values and capabilities. Things turned uglier before getting better as there were attempts to vote Jenny off the board. Secret meetings were held when she was out of the country, misrepresentation of facts, and true attempts to sabotage her. She claims to have had a "freak out" moment but was determined to rebuild or shut down. Engaging the community and mentors/advisors was a brilliant move as it was the strength of the project. From there, a working board was formed. After just one year, she was able to hire Lisa, who has helped tremendously to rebuild the business. "Sometimes, it takes hitting rock bottom," she says.

Mentorship vs. Sponsorship –what is the difference?

Mentor has experience and is there for guidance, will not execute much, and acts somewhat as an "entrepreneurial therapist." While a sponsor opens doors for you. They are in a position of power and will to share the power with you. Jenny shares that sponsors actually showed up for her when she was hitting hurdles in buying the building and was short on funding. "I believe in what you are doing," said one sponsor who came on and did a significant amount of work.

Who has contributed or what has contributed to your success more than anything?

Shannon Scutari, a mentor, sponsor, huge supporter, good friend, and co-chair of the foundation.

Francine Hardaway who had been involved in real estate, a real "fireball" one with whom she did not see eye-to-eye with at first but has become one of her greatest cheerleaders. She has a community focus and amazing mindset.

If you had to do something all over again, good or bad, what would it be?

Set up meetings with folks who fund projects.

If we are to make strides towards Fortune's goal of 100X25, we must:

Implement women friendly policies. As women and part of the general population, there must be better policies to support women to include enhanced childcare and access to good education for children. While there are more women graduating from college, fewer are in higher level positions. There are cultural challenges and system biases in larger companies. So, these organizations must consider their biases when developing policies and offering benefits. Sponsorship. Creating true sponsorship opportunities where other women are willing to put their name on the line.

Essential daily or weekly reads:

Reading six books right now – studies of leadership and innovation

Phoenix Business Journal

Favorite book of all times and why?

The Giver

Favorite quote?

"Always give first…start with giving" (who said this?)

When I am not working, I am:

Playing with her daughter.

If I could redo/relive a professional moment, it would be:

A few years ago, Jenny was asked to be on stage with Senator McCain and Governor Ducey. "I think I did fine, but I would have had better responses and spent more time with Senator McCain."

When you get comfortable in a position, it is time to move to another. Failure is NOT an option!

Sarah Boeder

Executive Vice President, Grand Canyon University

Best childhood memories.

When asked to describe her childhood memories, without hesitation, Sarah emphasizes the word "involved." From a very young age, it was evident to her that her family was poor, which caused a tremendous amount of stress for her mother. To avoid telling her parents that she was in fact eight months pregnant at the end of her senior year in high school, her mother moved to Phoenix. The tumultuous life continued, resulting in numerous marriages seeking solitude. "Having a guy was super important to her." That is probably why Sarah vowed to "never let a man run my life, I will always provide, won't rely on others for financial stability." All of this led to accelerated maturity and responsibility by Sarah taking a job, going grocery shopping, stocking the refrigerator, and helping with her siblings, thus acquiring a habit of hard work and responsibility at a young age and no doubt contributing to becoming an executive at a very young age. It is important to note that Sarah's determination to impart values to her children have become a sticking point with her family. "They believe that I am too religious, an extremist because I am trying to raise my children the way God wants them to be raised."

Favorite games to play growing up? Do any of those relate to who you are or what you do today?

Teacher and house were the favorites when growing up. However, teacher was the preferred way to spend time because "knowing something and sharing with someone else" gives life purpose. "I can absolutely see how that translates to my current position and definitely impacts my drive…why I do what I do."

From the movie Fallen, can you define what moment this was for you?

There were two moments Sarah mentioned as life changing. Knowing where you are and are not supposed to be can require significant shifts and leaps of faith in your life. The first, leaving ASU law school in the middle of the first semester. While the decision was admirable, it was costly. She had been awarded scholarships, all of which she had to pay back. Second, after working for University of Phoenix for years, she was offered the opportunity to move over to Grand Canyon University…for a pay cut. "I knew I was not supposed to be there." Not long after transitioning, she was given a significant increase, confirming that she had made the right move.

What jobs or experiences contributed the most to your success? Why?

Treating each opportunity as valuable is important, to not miss the learning that each position brings forth. No matter the position, from early years to executive, "Each was purposeful, prompting me to give 1000%." Pushing yourself beyond limits is important in the tedious of tasks or highly visible projects. Hence, being where you are meant to be…operating with purpose, on purpose decision-making, all leading to walking in purpose.

If your career could be told in a story, what would be the conflict, climax, and the antagonist, and what do you project to be a happy ending?

"I never asked for any of this!" She mentions being constantly surprised by promotions. "It's as though you are being set up for magnificence when doing your best where you are."

What did you do differently from colleagues to get to where you are?

I took risks, but ones with inner peace." It is important that you have inner peace. Sarah then recalls an event where she was called into the CEO/President's office and said to herself, "I'm being fired, I'm devastated." She told herself, "Whatever you do, don't cry. This has to be some horrible mistake in your file." President Mueller, an incredible man and leader, had scheduled a meeting with Sarah. He began the meeting by stating, "We've been reviewing your file and there is some horrible mistake." President Mueller went on to compliment Sarah on her hard work, letting her know he recognized that she had been stepping up in all kinds of ways.

What does Grit mean to you?

Sarah describes grit as perseverance, the ability to work through difficulty, and finally staying tough. It is essential, according to Sarah, to keep an edge, although "things, situations" are rubbing up against you. She recalls a day recently when her husband was undergoing surgery. "The kids were crying, and I know if it was me, no one would care." Jeff, being the primary caregiver, has developed a deep and different bond with the children over time. Certainly, a teacher, educator, and good with children, she has transformed through the process of taking care of the children.

What characteristics of grit do you possess?

"Confidence gained by the time I reached college." Sarah reflects on a time in high school. "I would go to the library at lunch because I was so embarrassed by my life. She realized in those moments that her life at the time was not a reflection of who she really was but her situation. This transformative thinking spurred her determination to attend college by saving for a semester, then earning straight A's, leading to a scholarship all while working three jobs: florist, front desk, and bookkeeper. She remembers telling herself, "I will make it!"

Excellence versus perfection is, according to Sarah, a point of refinement. Perfection limits and excellence extends.

What are your grittiest moments to date?

The outward appearance often indicates what is occurring on the inside. Sarah's changing exterior, her loss of hair and weight, did not fully align with what was manifesting internally. Changes to her physical appearance were tremendous, resulting in preconceived assumptions and diagnosis of cancer by those with whom she was not familiar. Perhaps it would have been easy to isolate, but no matter what, she had to remain strong, and it was difficult because what was said about her external appearance begin impacting the inside, her thinking. However, she was able to gain strength through the Bible and authentic discussions that helped to normalize what was happening. Ultimately, she describes seeing beauty in different things by not letting the illness have power "over me." To demonstrate the power, she spoke at a women's conference despite what she calls an "identity crisis," resulting in patches of missing hair. We would later spend tremendous amounts of time laughing about how she went to unsavory parts of the city to get her hair cut without fear or hesitation.

Mentorship vs. Sponsorship –what is the difference?

While Sarah does not currently have any formal mentorship relationships in place, she says that "people who know me come to me for truth!" You must be able to handle her mentorship, as she is known for truth-telling as she told one friend. "Change your attitude." Life is not about how we feel. "You don't do what you feel but what needs to be done. At that point, doors fly open and blessings are sure to follow."

Did/do you have a sponsor, coach, or mentor? If so, what do you believe is the most valuable information you have gleaned or help you were given?

Her mom gave her an impeccable work ethic. It is important to know what hard work looks like. Other shaping was the result of informal networks and people playing important roles in my life through different seasons of my life. Coaching is a critical component of success, of improvement, and of rising to the executive level. This became even more apparent as she described her "Tidbits of Wisdom," personal rules that she has created for herself.

- You cannot focus on feelings and what they tell us; they are often wrong.
- You have to lose to gain. If you're focused on the losing for the sake of gaining, the loss stops.
- Living out spiritual principles: serve to lead, humble to empower, do what needs to be done, give to receive, tear down to guard

- You don't do what you feel but do what needs to be done and doors fly open and blessings are right there.

What are some words of wisdom and no-nonsense advice you have received?

I don't let words deposit in me. There are truths I believe, and I focus on those. Wisdom – let others step up and trust that they will. Wisdom: "A few close friends are what you need" and those are the ones I allow to see me in a state of frustration. You can find strength and wisdom in the unlikeliest of places, and influences have purpose. See purpose in every job and every person, as there are no unnecessary details.

What is the greatest difference between you and your male counterpart, if any?

Guys can get away with things, all kinds of things. So much so that there is more tolerance for men's frustration level and corresponding behavior, while if I'm frustrated, I'm a witch.

If you had to do something all over again, good or bad, what would it be?

Sarah's very intentional. "I know what I want the outcome to be, which can make me hard to work with, as I have not always used the best approach to execute. However, being vulnerable is the best approach to working with people."

If we are to make strides towards Fortune's goal of 100X25, we must...

This is super sad. If we are to make strides, we have to be more cognizant. At times, we as women can be distracted by things that do not matter long term, and it gets in the way of us doing our very best. We must be willing to adapt as we do in our various roles of wife, mother, executive Sometimes women are not as aware of their climate, making it difficult to be seen as an equal. Again, being adaptable is essential. For example, men speak sports, therefore we sometimes have to enter the world of sports trying to understand who they are. There can be an assumption that women come in judging, complaining, and not adaptive. The good thing is that women connect emotionally, giving them the ability to connect.

What do women need to do more of to reach the highest levels in corporate America or beyond?

Chill out and focus on what is most important.

Ask yourself, "Are these the things leaders/executives are focused on as well?" We have to remember to not allow the wrong things to suck us in or distract us.

What do women need to do less of to reach the highest levels or corporate America?

If you treat people the way you want the outcome to be, you will win.

Favorite movie of all time and why?

"The Blind Side" – I love it! The family saw the potential, took him in as their own. This is what God does for us. We are not our best, but takes us and makes us feel loved, having what we need. Everything we do reflects love.

Favorite book of all time and why?

After the Bible, World War II books, stories of people living in that time and what they went through.

When I am not working, I am:

Cooking or lazy in a hammock, reading.

When I was at a low point, even my lowest point, it was important that I do ____to survive:

It was important that I not give up hope and I treat people like they love me anyway.

If I could redo/relive a professional moment, it would be...

The NASDAQ moment when Grand Canyon University broke the drought. I got to know the people who signed onto the project where they would possibly not reap benefits for years.

Best piece of business advice I ever received came from ______ and was_____:

President Brian Mueller of GCU, "Anyone can have an idea...very few can execute, fewer have perfect execution."

Dawn Venable

Engineering Leader, Hewlett Packard

Best childhood memories.

My happiest times were playing outdoors in the summertime in South Chicago where "we lived below my grandmother in an apartment complex."

Favorite games to play growing up? Do any of those relate to who you are or what you do today?

Adjacent to the complex was an empty lot where a number of street games were played, including Mother May I, tag, and hide and seek with a varying age range of children. However, a great deal of the fun came from creating "our own games." This set the foundation of inclusivity and creativity, valuing everyone's contribution and advancing collaboration.

From the movie Fallen, can you define what moment this was for you?

Going away to college. Knowing the selected college could affect her career, she chose to attend college in Tucson, Arizona, at the University of Arizona, where she would study engineering and begin her career at IBM, her first engineering job. Part of the experience involved living in an apartment with other women pursuing engineering, with whom she is still friends, as the experience led her to realize that "I could move anywhere and do anything. I knew I should venture out." This realization led Dawn to take a position in California, at the age of 22, after graduating from college.

What jobs or experiences contributed the most to your success? Why?

Career began as a team of four, male and female, working on low-cost printer circuit assembly under new product development for which a U.S. patent was granted.

Starting at 24 years of age, success was the direct result of achieving something that boosted all confidence. She was involved in chemical aspects, which pushed her outside of her comfort zone, and she then presented her work at the first HP women's conference.

If someone else were to tell about your accomplishments, what would they say? What would the list entail?

After becoming the technical lead, she moved the manufacturing of printer mechanism to a third party, a non-HP property. Design engineers are not necessarily popular to "train" engineers from another company. Following successful implementation of major projects, Dawn ended her career as an Engineering Project Manager accountable for product test development and implementation worldwide for the HP all-in-one printer. This was a home-grown product with a multi-geographical team. While she formally reported to the Operations functional area, she matrixed to Research & Development, leveraging testing into manufacturing processes. When placed in that role, it was unpopular due to the merging of test teams into one team. The business goal was to create one test team, converge processes, and unite test platforms.

What did you do differently from colleagues to get to where you are?

I really needed to connect with the team to earn their trust and support. It was a constant reminder that to get the job done, I needed to connect with them. Effective listening skills, which were enhanced through an HP survey that she conducted post-project implementation, asking team members related to the project what went well and where there were areas of improvement. She then sought one-on-one feedback from peers and upper management. Shortly following, she was promoted to engineering management.

Who or what has been your greatest inspiration?

Inspiration came from an early age. She experienced the loss of her grandparents and father at the age of 13. That is when she realized that "If I wanted to achieve something, I had to rely on myself." Her mother was emotionally unavailable due to the loss of her husband and own mother within six months of one another. "I had nothing to lose, had lost so much, so it is important to just go for it…go for things when you want something."

Which grit characteristics do you possess the most of and the least of?

Courage and conscientiousness early in my career. Now and towards the end, resilience: optimism, confidence, and creativity.

How long or how many experiences did it take to ascertain this characteristic of grit/grittiness?

By facing and overcoming obstacles, particularly when feeling "on my own, helped me to acquire courage to move on."

What are your grittiest moments to date?

Some of the grittiest moments in Dawn's career occurred while working on the East coast in Quality Improvement and supporting analytical efforts. She describes having to put her foot down to shift the culture. A culture where engineers needed to understand how manufacturing impacted product design. She was told, "My designs are fabulous; there is, comparatively, a small amount of field failures." She had support from leadership to create a more robust product design process which resulted in unbelievable improvement from 50% call rate to below 20%, maybe 17-18%. Critical to success is understanding how team members view the goals, but also how they are feeling and overall having mutual respect. In her case, they focused on the quality of the product, common vision and purpose, common ground with the foundation of open-mindedness, empathy, and willingness to listen.

What has been your greatest winning accomplishment so far?

"I was put in a position to use my talents, a highly visible position with support. It was a very tough assignment that involved ISO certification leadership and a brand-new all-in-one factory from

Europe to the Netherlands and the responsibility to represent." Dawn was chosen from the Executive Management program.

Mentorship vs. Sponsorship –what is the difference?

More sponsorship than mentorship. When recommended for special projects, be available. This primarily came from one female manager (as you can imagine, engineering was very male dominated). Dawn paid it forward by becoming a good sponsor immediately upon going into management.

What are some words of wisdom and no-nonsense advice you have received?

Words of wisdom came from a male manager who encouraged to show more emotion…you don't need to scale back passion or emotion. The worst advice, interestingly enough, was from a female who said to be more of a bull in a china shop, and "if someone gets offended, so be it."

What is the greatest difference between you and your male counterpart, if any?

Male counterparts tend to commit to something and have a confidence level without having all the data required. Conversely, I would commit, but only to a point and with caveats about needing and wanting more data. "I preferred to conduct more research and commit to dates when completing something."

If we are to make strides towards Fortune's goal of 100X25, we must…

Awareness and cultural shift targeting all levels of female students – high school and college specifically. Mentoring, key classroom projects, specific co-curricular activities, and early association with important organizations. Programs that assist in retention of female students the cultural change has to occur from the classroom to the boardroom.

Expectations and agility – there can be modifications made to roles; roles can be redefined and reshaped to give a variety of people access to different opportunities. Roles can become more tailored to support a greater opportunity for women to reach their career/life goal.

Is this possible in your industry...why?

This is where more thought and focus should be, as there are numerous studies that provide insight. Some studies cite women and men have varying career goals at times, primarily due to what is attractive and what brings the most satisfaction. Not all women want the top spot, according to Dawn, and she offers the question to other CEO's as to what companies can do to make the role or male-dominated industry of engineering, more attractive to the female executive?

Essential daily or weekly reads

Wall Street Journal

The Orange County Register

What do women need to do more of to reach the highest levels in corporate America or beyond?

Support each other more, advocate more. "When you hear stories from our daughters, it is clear that women are considered unsupportive of one another, which needs to change."

Favorite movie of all times and why?

"Life is Beautiful" with Robert Benigni – A World War II story, horrors of Nazi concentration camp where father and son are trapped, and the father is protecting the son, day-to-day. The father tries to help the son by getting him to view their experience at the camp as a game. Powerful.

Favorite book of all times.

Malcolm Gladwell - David & Goliath

Leif Enger – Peace Like a River

Favorite quote?

"There may be people who have more talent than you, but there is no excuse for anyone to work harder than you." Derek Jeter

When I am not working, I am:

Doing yoga

It is essential for women to know _____ and do _____:

It is essential for women to know they should give credit, but not be modest and do be courageous.

When I was at a low point, even my lowest point, it was important that I do _____to survive:

Her lowest point came during the death of her mother one year ago. Volunteering and going into the community helped her to deal with her loss.

People would be surprised if they knew I:

Survived the south side of Chicago…it doesn't come up in conversation often.

Kim McWaters, CEO

Universal Technical Institute (Retired)

Best childhood memories.

Kim grew up with extended family members: her aunt, grandmother and others. She grew up as the oldest of four children and felt very loved. She thoroughly enjoyed Christmas, special family dinners, and holidays.

What were your favorite games to play growing up? Do any of those relate to who you are or what you do today?

Roller skating, music, board games, tag, softball, and volleyball. I also liked playing grocery store and working with the cash register is probably closest to what I am doing today.

From the movie Fallen, can you define what moment this was for you?

Growing up, Kim describes herself as a "goodie two shoes" who played by the rules. She was raised in a religious home and became pregnant after high school. This began an unbelievable part of her life – conflict – should she have the baby? should she marry? One Sunday, she found herself in front of her church with approximately 2,000 eyes looking at her. She looked back at them and explained that she would be having the baby but not marrying the father. This was a tough but liberating moment that demonstrated tolerance versus judgement. At 18, she had the strength to face any audience…then and now. She has now become of champion of others who are faced with such difficult circumstances.

What jobs or experiences contributed the most to your success? Why?

Having been raised with strict parents, there was conflict even in their initial pro-life beliefs until their own daughter became pregnant. Her mother did not want to lose face, as she had become pregnant in her early years as well. It just so happened that her aunt and uncle knew the founder of UTI, Robert (Bob) Sweet. Her uncle would drive her to work every day. Bob was kind enough to give her a job on the switchboard. She spent time speaking with and consulting families – those that would visit the school and eventually graduate. That is when she realized that "I can make a difference here." The work she was doing was lifechanging, helping people change their circumstances. Prior to becoming pregnant with Nick, she had received a scholarship and was majoring in theatre, with an interest in sociology/social work. This work aligned very well with her interests, where she was promoted to an administrative clerical role. There was only one problem…she did not know how to type. In June 1984, Nick (her son) turned one year old, which corresponded with her 90-day review period, when it was realized that Kim had very good perspective on admissions.

If your career could be told in a story, what would be the conflict, climax, and the antagonist, and what do you project to be a happy ending?

Kim's trajectory began with answering phones, clerical, licensing/ regulatory positions where she was required to read all state regulations, which launched her into a compliance role, then onto Sales Management/Public Relations & Advertising. In the mid '90s, she was tasked with changing the perception of students, creating career paths, differentiating UTI, engaging industry, raising nobility, and brand validation. He would drive her and help her to understand the business, and she saw it as her job to help others understand how nice he was, yet most viewed him as rough, tough, and gruff.

If someone else were to tell about your accomplishments, what would they say? What would the list entail?

Kim was responsible for determining how to serve the customer differently, building brand value, and an architype. One who is a hero, a sage, one who answered the call that caused differentiation in our brand; one who was faced with significant barriers that overcame; one who has grit; one who took what they learned to improve the opportunities for other, particularly the underdog, which is part of her personal values.

What did you do differently from colleagues to get to where you are?

Focused on the need of the customer, end user, ultimately increasing/ improving our level of quality as an organization. That is what promoted Kim to president; grow outside of Phoenix and Houston; "fighting the good fight and motivating differently."

Building a differentiated company while creating a cultural shift, which involves taking on the fight of others; becoming the voice for the underdog; and repositioning ourselves as the beneficiary as a result of prioritizing customers (students).

What does Grit mean to you?

Having been a prior athlete, she visually sees an athlete, exhausted and sweating, but determined to win. Seeing the whole picture as an opportunity to win; as a track star is exhibiting tremendous amounts of endurance; passion when exhausted, but truly with purpose and a huge desire not to disappoint.

Which characteristics do you possess the most of and the least of?

Courage and resilience, which adds purpose and passion to "everyday work," which requires you to be vulnerable and willing to fail, causing you to believe so strongly in something.

How long or how many experiences did it take to ascertain this characteristic of grit/grittiness?

Thinking and talking with trusted friends to provide validation. As a woman, you cannot spend too much energy in the negative, which requires you to talk yourself back up, "game on."

What are your grittiest moments to date?

During very challenging economic times, we were required to restructure the organization to survive. It was very difficult, as I did not want to hurt people.

What has been your greatest winning accomplishment so far?

The ability to galvanize the team to transform the organization to a level of breakthrough performance. Kim engaged team members across UTI, formed project teams from the janitorial staff to department executives, resulting in tremendous cost savings and efficiencies, and allowing UTI to enter an IPO in 2003.

Mentorship vs. Sponsorship –what is the difference?

Robert (Bob) Suite, founder, was of course a sponsor, who emphasized, "Nothing happens until the sale is made, until a student is committed or enrolled." Some people may have a negative reaction, however, there is a win for the student as well as the organization. Bob Hartman, who is still alive, always says, "Nobody cares how much you know until they know how much you care."

What are some words of wisdom and no-nonsense advice you have received?

Encourage people to be who they are. Help them to find purpose, power, passion, and a path prompted by their natural talent. Without an emotional connection, there is no source of energy…treat people as if they are what they envision.

If we are to make strides towards Fortune's goal of 100X25, we must:

Have acknowledgement from employers. There must flexible policies and structures that support women. Currently, women must make a choice to have a family or career; they are faced with priorities and pressures from societal norms. Rather than having to start over, there should be opportunities for women to enjoy both.

Essential daily or weekly reads:

Read daily news nightly, flip around, but enjoy reading what people post on Facebook. Real life challenges and triumphs.

Favorite movie of all time.

"Pretty Woman" & "Love Actually"

Favorite book of all time.

Built to Last

Good to Great

The Nightingale – strength and courage of women

Favorite quote?

Bob Hartman – "Treat people as they wish to be seen and not as they are. They become the inspiration that you speak."

When I am not working, I am:

Relaxing with husband

Being outdoors at a musical event

People would be surprised if they knew I:

I wanted to be an actress and I am very introverted!

Sintra Hoffman, CEO
WESTMARC

Best childhood memories.

Family vacations, long weekends where parents took them on road trips. Using Triple AAA books, her parents would say, "Sintra, tell us where we are going and what are we going to see." She would always come up with something fun, even in Maryland.

Favorite games to play growing up? Do any of those relate to who you are or what you do today?

Sintra has a closeness with her family that still exist today and has a strong positive impact on her daughter. Most people fight in the car, but not this family. The group was very adventurous, looking for new experiences on the road, which is critical to who she is today. Games included Red Light, Green Light, and 1-2-3. Sintra was the oldest of three girls with numerous cousins who grew up with her as they all stayed in a multiple family dwelling.

From the movie "Fallen," can you define what moment this was for you?

The moment she decided to leave her marriage. "I spoke the with my husband at the time and there was no turning back." The family was attached to the ex…" did not realize I was cutting off my arm but was left with a portion of my body." At the same time, she lost her job at the City of Surprise. Everything changed in a matter of weeks, her entire foundation was rocked.

What jobs or experiences contributed the most to your success? Why?

Early in her career, during college, she worked for TWA, Piedmont, US Airways, and Korean Air. After graduating, she remained in the travel business, "always planning someone else's time."

Sintra studied Marketing in undergraduate and obtained a Master's in Public Administration after having a child.

If your career could be told in a story, what would be the conflict, climax, and the antagonist, and what do you project to be a happy ending?

The City of Surprise situation was very painful. There was conflict, and difficulty and occurred in conjunction with the separation. All resulted in a complete loss of identity. We identify ourselves with our profession. Everything goes back to the foundation of our career. After Surprise, ADOT. There was a new mayor in Surprise. I was on the top floor and ended up being dusted out like a dust bunny. I got swept out. I served six years as Assistant Division Director where I oversaw public affairs, working with the local community and business. I was then recruited. This would be my career climax when I was made CEO of WESTMARC. The role was stressful, every job has an impact then changes/growth occurs. I worked on the City of Surprise physical infrastructure, which included 726 new contacts for the agency, 3000 square miles of communities, and 12 different cities, representing all on economic development issues/opportunities.

The climb to success – If someone else were to tell about your accomplishments, what would they say? What would the list entail?

Getting her master's degree in 1999 then moved to the Arizona city of Surprise as Assistant to the City Manager. Responsible for planning, budgeting while serving on the Arts & Cultural Advisory Board. Sintra was then promoted to Government Relations Director, responsible for transportation – Loop 303, worked with Arizona Department of Transportation in every step of the planning. Best accomplishments, being promoted to Deputy City Manager and securing a commercial residential development agreement. Knowing how to build arsenic treatment plant. Grow an economy, funding and infrastructure plans including water, sewer, other associated infrastructure. Surprise Point which is now "crescent crown" and she negotiated the deal. Councilmen she worked with were all men. "The guys took the fire out of my belly." Every morning this is the best thing. Day 30 things adjusted and so did her body. It really was the best thing: seven stages of grief within seven days.

What did you do differently from colleagues to get to where you are?

"The drive in me…the New Yorker in me," which she attributes to her father. Her dad would say, "Work hard and you will have anything you want in life" …to my detriment at times, it resulted in professional jealousy.

Who or What has been your greatest inspiration?

Sintra described her own personality as strong and she realizes she needs to own it. People always perceived her as bossy and her father's words of wisdom have continued to inspire her so much so, she stood to read the "Dadisms" at his 75th birthday where she choked up. Her daughter sees this reaction and is impacted as well. Mother was the inspiration. She was a mover and shaker. She is outgoing, friendly, people love her. She takes from her building relationships as she has relationships with everyone. Her success is attributed to both of her parents.

Excellence vs. Perfection. Which of these do you possess the most of and the least of?

Sintra describes herself as a perfectionist who always needed to work. She raised her 23-year-old daughter and went from government retirement to WESTMARC. On the downside, "I take too much on my plate." Sintra has spent the greatest amount of time working most on resilience and excellence/perfection. "I see myself able to make anything happen."

Stories of female grit...your grittiest moments to date?

During her work with ADOT, she was working with a city engineer regarding the implementation of the red-light running camera. The mayor signed a letter and had Maricopa Association of Government support (MAG) but refused to issue the permit. The City Manager, Government Relations, advised them that they were being unfair, and their decision was in conflict with the regional approach. She was beat up, bloody in battle, climbing the hill. After not giving up, the engineer contacted her to say, "We'll issue the permit." The engineer joined in the fight and went to a meeting. He said it was quite contentious and said he got his "ass kicked." He said, "You were so staunch in your position and all cities ended up supporting the plan." That is why, according to Sintra, it is critical to have people standing behind you. That way, "You can get quiet when you get angry…that is what I must do."

"I want every one of you to become the subject of someone else's story of overcoming." What does this mean to you?

Sintra's Dad says, "Sintra, some people listen, and some have to feel and experience things on their own. I've learned to listen." Her friend for 12 years of age reminded her that "you have to know things, a lot of different things. At times people will underestimate you so you will want to be pretty formal, yet friendly." Her friend went on to remind her of her excellent business development skills, great work she had done on an environmental study, and effort to improve the percentage of arsenic in the water.

What is the greatest difference between you and your male counterpart, if any?

Parental tough love. Evaluation of women in these positions is very different. There is strong residual of "boys' network." Conversely, West Valley was different - fast changing, shifting from old world and politically focused, where male counterparts have the luxury of a network.

If you had to do something all over again, good or bad, what would it be?

Arizona was the fifth move for her daughter, as Sintra was ready to begin her career. She wished she had the patience to be a part-time mom and wait an additional year before sending her to school full-time. This would have made for an easier transition from Germany to

Arizona. Sintra was born in Trinidad and had an immigrant mindset and work ethic. That is where the grit comes from.

If we are to make strides towards Fortune's goal of 100X25, we must:

More mentorship. "Early in careers, we saw women who hated their position and lack of positioning." Sintra did mentioned that it had been 10 years since she's been formally connecting, which is what she would like to do more of.

Is this possible in your industry...why?

Yes. Mentoring needs to be more structured and so does sponsorship. It is important to begin "pitching and promoting" one another. Start having and leveraging conversations with both mentors and sponsors. Also, to be successful, we do need to engage white men over 50 years of age, getting them to embrace women and the difference and develop the talent.

Essential daily or weekly reads...

Arizona Republic – "My world is political" and the Phoenix Business Journal

What do women need to do more of to reach the highest levels in corporate America or beyond?

Be more open to learning different areas. Continue with your passion. Limit some of your assignments to one to two years, grow out of that, then take more areas. Too many of us don't become fully proficient. It is critical to add tools to your toolbox so that you can get things across the finish line.

Favorite movie of all time and why?

"Romancing the Stone" – different place, different personalities, and coming together. "Shawshank Redemption" – fighting and will power.

Favorite book of all time and why?

Water for Elephants – Read every single word from front to back cover. Hard life for carnival people, the struggle, decision parents made to give up kids …very raw.

Favorite quote?

Her dad would say, "Work hard and you will have anything you want in life."

When I am not working, I am:

Working out

People would be surprised if they knew I:

Was born in Trinidad, moved to New York, and am an open book, even though people assume I would not be.

Best piece of business advice I ever received came from?

A former City Manager was recruiting an executive for the city, and Sintra was not keeping him in the loop. "We were different, and I had to learn to communicate as we had different styles which led to a lack of understanding one another." Sintra said that she could not understand why he didn't love her. Then she looked in the mirror and realized that the burden of communication was on her and she needed to "get the smoke out of her ears." "You have to own your shortcomings and be committed to getting better. Similarly, if you see talent, you have to say the hard words." The gentleman mentioned above ended up promoting Sintra twice. People are making an investment in you, and you should pass along the investment.

Susan L. Brooks, CEO

Best childhood memories.

My refined, stylized, and courageous grandmother was my light and greatest teacher. She provided a happy safe space for me to grow. As a very successful businesswoman, long before it was acceptable and supported to be successful in business as a woman, Edith Irma Siegel was a trailblazer in the interior design industry, often referred to as the design industry's matriarch. I learned core values and principles from her example that I still use in my work every day: Your clients are your friends. And my favorite, "Often, getting dressed is the best part of the day!" She remained a powerful influence with my every decision in growing Cookies from Home into a multi-million-dollar company.

What jobs or experiences contributed the most to your success? Why?

Serving as a high school English teacher contributed to my growth and success as a human being. I taught twelfth grade English in a time where education followed a specified curriculum using a state-adopted textbook. I was an entrepreneur and maverick to my colleagues, especially my principal, when I realized I needed to engage my students in a new and different way of learning. The old ways just wouldn't work, and the curriculum didn't reflect what these kids needed. I created an innovative curriculum that invited students to get excited about reading to see the timeless relevancy of English literature to their own lives. Transformation was a thrill. I think being a teacher has always been my foundation to serve, no matter what else I did as a business owner or business coach…it's always about teaching for me.

If someone else were to tell about your accomplishments, what would they say? What would the list entail?

Throughout my professional life, I am best known for my hard work ethic, innovative solutions, resourceful connections, integrity and authenticity, and on-going pursuit to serve. These qualities show up in the high school classroom; the creation, management, and growth of a multi-million dollar and award-winning cookie company; and my passion to serve other women business owners, world-wide and throughout the nation and my Phoenix community.

Who or what has been your greatest inspiration?

My greatest inspiration is to serve in ways that matter, where my contribution impacts lives, both personally and professionally. Powerful women, starting with my grandmother, inspire me as living proof of what's possible. I live for results.

What has been your greatest winning accomplishment so far?

My husband of 51 years makes me proud. He teaches Zumba to seniors. Our children are wildly successful; both are entrepreneurs themselves. Our son is a financial advisor and our daughter a therapist. I am proud of the ability to start a company from scratch, growing and selling an iconic brand that generated the success of a multi-million-dollar company. I'm grateful to the 3,000 people who worked with us over our 30 years in business. We made an impact with our clients and ultimately made a difference in the community. Today, I am most proud of the women business owners I am privileged to serve, using my skills and expertise from having been in the trenches.

Mentorship vs. Sponsorship –what is the difference?

A mentor invests in you, cares about you and your journey, your success. I'm currently serving as part of the venture development program at ASU Entrepreneurs program. I'm invested in these young entrepreneurs and care about their success. In 2010, after we sold Cookies from Home, I went to China and taught a 6-8-week leadership class at an international university. I worked with young girls and their families, helping them to become global leaders. Sponsors write a check to a cause.

Did/do you have a sponsor, coach, or mentor? If so, what do you believe is the most valuable information you have gleaned or help you were given?

Find a coach who you have synergy with and who specializes in the expertise you need. There isn't a one size fits all. For example, I'm a growth strategist and I work with female entrepreneurs who are seeking ways to grow their business. They have something they believe in and don't know how to grow it. Sometimes women believe they must do it all themselves, and with a coach, you gain so much insight and accountability, and create a roadmap so that you don't have to get stuck in fear or overwhelm. I could have really used a coach when I was growing my company. We did have male consultants who would help us solve specific problems, like inventory systems or financial processes. However, when I chose a sales meeting over a parent-teacher school conference, there was little support and validation for my conflicted resolution.

What are some words of wisdom and no-nonsense advice you have received?

A leader is tested to the core and must have core values. If a leader is seeking convenience, money, or just working against deadlines versus the right thing to do, the leader will have many challenges.

What is the right thing to do, regardless of the circumstances? When you think no one is looking, that is when everyone is watching you.

Love the work that needs to get done: your spirit is counting on you!

The ultimate customer experience is your differentiator.

Grit means getting in the trenches and doing the right thing to get the work done

Be fierce…on purpose.

How I stay grounded: Meditate every day, exercise 3-5X a week, eat healthy foods, and surround myself with flowers, beauty, and good friends who fuel my soul. My women friends speak truth to me. Nature is always a way for me to reconnect and stay grounded, whether it's sitting by the ocean or hiking a dense green forest. Beauty is oxygen for me.

Favorite movie of all time and why?

"King of Hearts" with Alan Bates. Unfortunately, it can't be found today, though its message is more relevant than ever. I used this film when I was teaching about the perils of war to promote an anti-war society. It's provocative still.

Favorite book of all time and why?

It is easier for me to identify my favorite and often-read authors: Maya Angelou, Brene Brown, Paulo Coelho, Seth Godin, Anne Lamott, and Tom Robbins.

Favorite quote?

Rumi, "Don't be a spectator on this trip. There is no death worse than just waiting around. Set your heart on the Hero's Gold…and GO."

When I am not working, I am:

Luxuriating in the present moment, either with my children or grandchildren…or private moments with my husband, always in gratitude for my blessed life.

It is essential for women to know _____ and do _____:

Be Brave. Believe in your Self. Serve with all your heart. Most importantly, recognize you don't have to do it all alone. Enroll, engage, delegate others to give you the support you need to grow.

People would be surprised if they knew:

The depth of the challenges in my life. My persistence and perseverance remind me often of my own strength, courage, and resilience.

Best piece of business advice I ever received came from ______ and was_____:

"There is no greater gift than to honor my calling. It's why I was born…and how I become most truly alive." This quote reminds me every day to choose, to step up…and to step out to serve others. In business, showing up fully, taking risks, honoring my intention: these are the qualities that helped me grow a multi-million-dollar business!

Pam Gaber, CEO

Founder Gabriel's Angels

Best childhood memories.

I was an active child and loved riding my bike and playing in the dirt! My bicycle gave me freedom and independence. I loved our pets, which included a dog and a cat. I recall the laughter when our orange tabby would attack my mother's feet as she was trying to make the bed! The sheets and her feet were fair game! Overall, my mother was a fun person and was the first to purchase me a chemistry set so I could conduct experiments. After a big mishap, she decided outdoor activities were better for me. So, I took up butterfly catching!

What were your favorite games to play growing up? Do any of those relate to who you are or what you do today?

I loved playing tag with my friends. I felt it was a fun challenge, and if someone was slow or tired, I could let them tag me. I was competitive but helpful. I see myself as that to this day, as I always want to do my best but not at the expense of others. We are all better off working together!

What jobs or experiences contributed the most to your success? Why?

I spent seven years teaching Veterinary Technology at a Jr. College. I then began working for a pharmaceutical company in their Animal Health Division. That career lasted fifteen years, and I gained valuable business and leadership experience. As you can see, I spent twenty-two years working directly and indirectly with animals. My business experience has enabled me to run Gabriel's Angels as a business, not a passionate hobby. I contribute this to my success running a sustainable nonprofit.

If your career could be told in a story, what would be the conflict, climax, and the antagonist, and what do you project to be a happy ending?

In my corporate career, the conflict was balancing a male-dominated industry with my desire to succeed. I positioned myself as an equal, not a lower ranking peer. I focused on the bigger picture, which was to be successful in my job.

If someone else were to tell about your accomplishments, what would they say? What would the list entail?

Starting a nonprofit agency with the belief that it would succeed. The persistence to see things through as well as an upbeat positive attitude contributed to the success of Gabriel's Angel's.

What did you do differently from colleagues to get to where you are?

I believe in the concept first stated in Malcolm Gladwell's book, Outliers, which says that anyone can master a skill with 10,000 hours of practice. I was never afraid to put in the time to master anything I was inspired to master. That being said, these are things that are attainable and not pie in the sky. I could never train enough hours to be a superstar basketball player due to my 5'5" height.

Who or what has been your greatest inspiration?

My greatest inspiration was and continues to be our founding dog, Gabriel. He was the reason I started the agency. Once I saw the impact, he had on the children residing at Crisis Nursery in Phoenix. On the days when I thought to myself, "Can I do this?", I would look at the gentle gray dog staring intently into my eyes while wagging his tail, and I knew that together we could. Gabriel's Angels is Gabriel's legacy, and my staff and I work incredibly hard to ensure the agency continues to serve vulnerable children.

What does Grit mean to you?

I read Angela Duckworth's book when it first came out after I read a review about it. The book resonated with me as I said to myself, "This is it! It is the term for persevering in the face of adversity and never giving up." To me, grit is the one term that embraces all that makes one successful such as creating a village of support, having kick ass resilience, and being willing to change your course of direction for the greater good.

Which characteristics do you possess the most of and the least of?

I would say my number one characteristic that I have is resilience. I define resistance as coming out of adversity in better shape than when you went into the difficult situation. Many circumstances in life test us, and rather than have the hard ones bring us down, there is always something to be learned. Victimization is not a sign of strength!

I have done serious work in striving for excellence vs striving for perfection. It was a hard lesson, as I was a typical overachiever that also had to be perfect. Over the years, I have learned that perfectionism is seriously overrated as you rarely learn anything from being perfect.

How long or how many experiences did it take to ascertain this characteristic of grit/grittiness?

I learned grit early as a young girl. When someone told me I couldn't do it, my first reaction was, "Watch me!" This didn't always work out as planned, but I learned a lot!

What are your grittiest moments to date?

Perhaps starting a nonprofit agency (Gabriel's Angels) was my grittiest move to date. A nonprofit startup success rate mirrors the for-profit sector, in that approximately only 3% will make it to the fifth year. It took an immense amount of courage to start from scratch in a niche (pet therapy for abused and neglected children) that did not exist eighteen years ago. I did not have any model I could utilize for success. In addition to creating the model, I had to create momentum to educate people on this new concept. People had heard about therapy dogs in hospitals and nursing homes but not healing children in crisis.

It also took an immense amount of endurance to keep my eye on the long-term vision while growing Gabriel's Angels. You do all you can in the beginning as you never know when something will pop. I now have a better sense of what to do and what not to do to ensure sustainability but being picky up front would have been a detriment to our growth.

And finally, my resilience, spirit, and hardiness were major factors in our success in the beginning. Now that I have mobilized supporters, board members, and staff, we have a sustainable model to ensure we can provide our services to Arizona children.

My other gritty moments were the six marathons I have completed. I learned the immense power of my brain to push through when I thought I could not. How do you run a marathon? One step at a time! It speaks to how we get through anything in life…a step at a time. This strengthened my mental fortitude to accomplish whatever I put my mind to.

What has been your greatest winning accomplishment so far?

This would be building a successful nonprofit that will be here well beyond Gabriel and me. While my heart and soul are in this agency, it would have been an ego-based move to make it about me. Ten, 20, even 50 years from now, a very few will know who the founder was. They will remember the impact Gabriel's Angels has in the community. That is my ultimate mission.

Mentorship vs. Sponsorship –what is the difference?

I am not sure you can be one without being the other, although some research says differently. A mentor is there to listen, advise, and support their mentee. A mentor may also advocate for their mentee, as that is a natural byproduct of the relationship. Being a sponsor who simply advocates for a protégé must be involved in some type of mentoring if they are to be successful in advocating for their protégé. In this instance, it is like a referral that you make because you know the person and are thereby putting your reputation on the line. It has to be more than just promoting your protégé to the executive team.

Did/do you have a sponsor, coach, or mentor? If so, what do you believe is the most valuable information you have gleaned or help you were given?

I have had many coached and mentors, as I am enjoying hearing other people's point of view and understanding how their experiences shaped their opinions and value systems.

How did you find your sponsor, coach, or mentor?

I find them within my network. I watch and listen to their words, behavior and actions. If I feel they are all aligned, I approach them to meet for coffee to ascertain how we can help each other.

Who has contributed or what has contributed to your success more than anything?

My persistence and authenticity have helped me along the way. I am not afraid to ask for feedback in situations where I want to know more but I am not afraid to make decisions on my own. I am able to see the big picture and not get caught up in the minutia.

"I want every one of you to become the subject of someone else's story of overcoming."

What does this mean to you?

It means that I have been a good role model to someone on staying on course and not getting distracted. That I have maintained my focus throughout the journey and embraced mistakes as an awesome way of learning!

What are some words of wisdom and no-nonsense advice you have received?

I believe that failure is one of the best teachers. If we always succeed, it means we did not stretch ourselves to perform better. Perfection is the enemy of true progress. Humans are not infallible…we are imperfect beings on an imperfect journey.

What is the greatest difference between you and your male counterpart, if any?

Many men have the competitive spirit of winning at all costs. To win at others' expense is ego-based and not successful when looking at the big picture.

If you had to do something all over again, good or bad, what would it be?

I would start Gabriel's Angels all over again. While there was and continues to be a lot of required grit and belief, it has been the best experience of my life.

Can you describe the uniqueness of your role or a career relative to women?

The many women who have excelled in a male-dominated industry have had to develop the skills to interact and be successful with their male counterparts. The fact is, men do lead differently, women can be champions of other women, and all can work together.

If we are to make strides towards Fortune's goal of 100X25, we must…

Put more women in leadership roles, as they tend to hire more women as well as mentor them. This will take both men and women embracing diversity and acting upon it.

Is this possible in your industry...why?

The nonprofit sector ranks high with women in leadership positions. This may be due to the higher overall women employment numbers in the sector.

Essential daily or weekly reads:

Daily I read the Arizona Republic and the Wall Street Journal as well as any e-newsletters I receive such as Leadership IQ, BoardSource, and the Nonprofit Times.

Weekly I read the Phoenix Business Journal.

Monthly I read the Chronical of Philanthropy, Women's Health, and Oprah. All work and no play makes Pam a dull girl!

What do women need to do more of to reach the highest levels in corporate America or beyond?

Advocate for themselves and work hard. No ne reaches the pinnacle of their career without putting in the time and being an exceptional leader. Women excel at this, and I have great confidence in our younger generation!

What do women need to do less of to reach the highest levels or corporate America?

Women need to be less afraid to fail. Women need to be bold, daring, and willing to work hard and stay focused.

Favorite movie of all time and why?

I enjoy movies that captivate me, so any "Harry Potter" movies fit the bill.

Favorite book of all time and why?

I loved the book I just finished reading, which was Dare to Lead, by Berne Brown.

Favorite quote?

"Nobody made a greater mistake than she who did nothing because she could do only a little." Edmund Burke (edited by Pam to incorporate a female pronoun)

When I am not working, I am:

Trail running or hiking, as I love our mountains and desert! I also love to read a good book.

It is essential for women to know _______ and do ______:

It is essential for women to truly know WHO they are as well as to have the self-awareness of who we are NOT. We must embrace our feminine traits and never apologize for who we are. I hear women say "sorry" a lot in circumstances where that is not necessary. I am all for apologizing when necessary but not for everything. Also, my pet peeve is women and men who shake hands limply with another person. Aim for where the thumb and pointer meet, and this will ensure a strong handshake as you genuinely look into the other person's eyes. It forms a strong connection.

When I was at a low point, even my lowest point, it was important that I do _____to survive:

It is important that I believed in myself. That I held the belief that I was stronger than the situation and the belief in my ability to overcome it. "If it is going to be…it's up to me!" Wallowing in low points is simply unproductive. Also, the low points in our life is the catalyst for the next high point, as life is not a vertical line of events.

If I could redo/relive a professional moment, it would be:

I would relive the moment I walked into the ballroom of the hotel where we were hosting our largest event for 1,000 people prior to the doors opening. The size of the ballroom, the number of tables, and the overall ambiance literally blew me away. It was quiet in the room and I took it all in. I felt so very proud of Gabriel's Angels!

When equating my life and success to a real person or fictitious character, I would choose:

I admire many successful women who have inspired me with their tenacity, hard work, and pushing boundaries, not one single one that I could equate my life and success to. Here are the winners in the following categories:

Kindness – Ellen DeGeneres

Focus – Oprah Winfrey

Authenticity – Donna played by Meryl Streep in "Mama Mia 2"

People would be surprised if they knew I:

Despite my outgoing personality, I have the intense need to introvert to recharge my batteries. I am not the girl that is out every night because I don't like to be alone. I crave my "me time"!

Best piece of business advice I ever received came from ______ and was_____:

Early on when I started Gabriel's Angels, I was not comfortable with the "circle of philanthropy" in that it differed greatly from my experience in corporate America, where we had a product to sell and I understood the sales cycle. Philanthropy is different, as there is not a product or service received by the donor. I had a lot of anxiety on how to control this "sales cycle." I asked for a meeting with a gentleman who started Rancho Feliz, which was in its fifteenth year of service. Gil was listening to me talk about Gabriel's Angels, and he commented that everything I said sounded right on track. "So, what is the problem" he asked? I told him I felt that I had no control in creating financial stability for Gabriel's Angels. Some funds came from here, there, everywhere, and nowhere. His comment back to me was, "Get used to how money is raised in the nonprofit sector. Just go after all you can in the beginning and build strong grassroots following. Many times, the money will come from the place you least expected it." Eighteen years later, that was the best advice I could have received, as I took it to heart, and it put Gabriel's Angels on a successful trajectory.

Shannon Goldwater

Founder, Feeding Matters

Best childhood memories.

During the summer, we often drove to Kansas to visit extended family. During these long drives, I remember playing lots of different games in the car. One of my favorites was trying to get truck drivers to honk their horns back at me. I remember how excited I would get when I succeeded! I also remember I used to hate when my mom would put my hair in two perfect braids... a fact that now makes me smile every time I think about it.

Favorite games to play growing up? Do any of those relate to who you are or what you do today?

Growing up, I played Gin Rummy with my Dad, and I was a huge fan of the arcade game Centipede. My husband and I play backgammon nearly every day and even keep a detailed spreadsheet of our total wins and losses. I love playing games because it is a great way to have fun and connect with people. Also, it teaches us a very valuable life lesson at a very young age -- you don't always win!

From the movie "Fallen," can you define what moment this was for you?

I was completely unprepared as a first-time mom when my triplets were born four months prematurely, weighing just over one pound each and requiring feeding tubes to survive. For the first eight years of their lives, there was not a single meal where the mere sight, smell, or taste of food did not make them sick or cause them to choke, gag, or cry. Feeding them was an agonizing and painful experience that we all dreaded. Watching your child (or in my case, children) suffer several times a day every time they eat is incredibly painful. Mealtimes should be based on trust - a time when we bond and foster meaningful relationships with our infants and young children. When children are unable to eat, they cannot thrive cognitively, physically, socially, or emotionally, and they are at high-risk for lifelong complications. I felt helpless and robbed of the vital need to feed and nurture my children.

Locally there were very limited resources to help me - no centers, no best practices, and long waiting lists. When the triplets were three-and-a-half years old, we uprooted our family and moved to Virginia for four months to attend a feeding clinic. It felt like it was my last hope. While there, the triplets made significant progress and were doing well. However, shortly after being discharged, we had to wean them off a powerful appetite-inducing medication. As a result, my children regressed in their ability to eat by 50%. We were worse off than we had been before the move. It felt like one step forward, two steps back. Or in my case, three. It was devastating, and I felt defeated. But it also was when I had an epiphany. I realized that when my children felt good, they were internally motivated to eat. Who would ever want to eat if it was a painful and traumatic experience that made you sick?

My experience became a huge motivator, lighting a fire in me that I did not have before. I did not want any other families going through what we were going through. I did not want any more kids suffering like my kids were suffering. It was on this foundation that I started Feeding Matters, a non-profit whose mission is to further advances in pediatric feeding disorders by accelerating identification, igniting research, and promoting collaborative care for children and families.

What jobs or experiences contributed the most to your success? Why?

I have always had a type-A personality. Whether it was selling the most cookies in my brownie troop or being the first person in my immediate family to go to college, I consistently pushed myself to be my best. In high school, I attended Madeira, an all-girls boarding school in Virginia. The co-curriculum at Madeira provided experiential learning through weekly internships that focused on service, citizenship, and leadership. These opportunities honed my leadership skills, encouraged compassion, and instilled a sense of responsibility in me.

If your career could be told in a story, what would be the conflict, climax, the antagonist, and what do you project to be a happy ending?

The conflict is the emotional connection I have to Pediatric Feeding Disorder ("PFD"). While this connection is where my passion and motivation are derived from, I do not want it to interfere or cloud my judgment or ever personalize critical business decisions.

The climax, of course, would be the creation of Feeding Matters and the work that we do, who we are, and what we fight for. We are the only organization in the world that unites the concerns of families with the field's leading advocates, experts, and allied healthcare professionals to improve the system of care for pediatric feeding disorders. Since 2006, we have reached families and medical professionals from all 50 states and over 143 countries. We advocate for these kids, educate parents and professionals, support families, and fund research -- all to get PFD the recognition it needs and deserves. PFD is not as rare as you might think: More than one in 37 American children under age five receives a diagnosis of, and currently has, a pediatric feeding disorder.

The antagonist has always been the magnitude of PFD and the fact that we are the first organization of our kind doing anything like this. We are not just making a few tweaks here and there; rather, we are completely trailblazing and restructuring the entire system for how medical professionals diagnose and treat these children. It can feel like an insurmountable battle, like making small steps on a giant mountain, but every step gets us closer.

The happy ending is eventually creating a world where children with PFD will thrive. A world where children and their families have access to the services they need and where PFD will be as commonly known and understood as other childhood disorders. While we are still far away from that point, and the logistics of exactly how to do that are not always clear, every step we take brings us closer to that goal.

Stories of female grit...your grittiest moments to date?

In 2014, after a nearly a decade of Feeding Matters advocating for kids with feeding issues, I was still struggling to figure out how we could raise more awareness and make a bigger impact. The general public had a hard time understanding the prevalence and severity of the condition because they had never heard of it before. Beyond that, parents were still being blamed and told that their kids were picky eaters and would eat when they are hungry – which just isn't true.

Then, I woke up one morning and it suddenly dawned on me... the absence of a universally accepted term and stand-alone diagnosis was the root cause of the system issues that failed my children and continue to fail children to this day. Because the condition is seen as a symptom of over 300 other conditions (such as Autism, congenital heart defects, prematurity, and cystic fibrosis, to name a few), the severity of the issue is frequently overlooked. This has resulted in a lack of collaborative care and qualified providers, no educational path or generally accepted qualifications for what constitutes a feeding therapist, poor insurance coverage, and an overall lack of awareness from the general public. We needed a universally accepted term and diagnostic criteria, starting from ground zero. So that is what we set out to do!

What has been your greatest winning accomplishment so far?

Gathering over 17 world thought-leaders from various disciplines in the field of pediatric feeding to determine a name, definition, and diagnostic criteria for Pediatric Feeding Disorder. "Pediatric Feeding Disorder: Consensus Definition and Conceptual Framework" was published by the Journal of Pediatric Gastroenterology and Nutrition in January 2019. The paper declares Pediatric Feeding Disorder as the unifying name and stand-alone diagnosis for the broad spectrum of pediatric feeding struggles. It defines PFD as "impaired oral intake that is not age-appropriate and associated with medical, nutritional, feeding skill, and/or psychosocial dysfunction."

In August of 2020, the U.S. Center for Disease Control and Prevention officially approved Pediatric Feeding Disorder to be a stand-alone diagnostic code (R code) in the International Classification of Disease. This means that in just five years of collaborating with families and healthcare professionals, Feeding Matters was the catalyst to the stand-alone name, definition, and diagnosis of PFD – a condition so many before us have merely dismissed as a symptom of a different problem. Now we have the launching pad for Feeding Matters' advocacy agenda - creating best practices, access to federal funding for research, PFD screening at well-check visits, inclusive insurance coverage, accredited specialists, and so much more!

Mentorship vs. Sponsorship –what is the difference?

A mentor is someone you admire who is willing to share their knowledge, expertise, and unique experiences that can be transferable and helpful to your own. Sponsors are more intimately connected with your specific career path and give you unique insights in how to progress in your field. They are typically senior level executives who advocate for you behind closed doors, encourage and help direct your professional development, and introduce you to their spheres of influence.

Did/do you have a sponsor, coach or mentor? If so, what do you believe is the most valuable information you have gleaned or help you were given?

I have had several amazing mentors over the years, all of whom are women I deeply admire.

Denise Reznick, co-founder of Southwest Autism Research & Resource Center (SAARC)

Joan Lowell, Community Activist

Laura Grafman, Virginia Piper Trust and Honor Health Care Foundation

Jill Goldsmith, Executive and Leadership Coach

If you had to do something all over again, good or bad, what would it be?

I would be more intentional about slowing down and enjoying the present moment. It is so easy to get caught up in worrying about the future or regretting the past. The present is a gift!

If we are to make strides towards Fortune's goal of 100X25, we must:

We must do something similar to Bill Gates and Warren Buffett's "The Giving Pledge". I believe a commitment from several Fortune 500 companies to create cultures that sponsor women leaders would be incredibly powerful. In addition, an organized call to action from women all over the world would accelerate change.

What do women need to do more of to reach the highest levels in corporate America or beyond?

Focus on careers that spark your interests and fuel a passion within you so that every day feels like a Friday. Also, women need to build one another up by encouraging and empowering each other to do more than they believe they can. We must be flexible and adaptive because the world is changing quickly.

Essential daily or weekly reads:

The app "Motivation".

Favorite movie of all times and why?

I love the movie Shawshank Redemption. To me, this movie shows that hope and inspiration are possible in every situation, even the most challenging.

Favorite book of all times and why?

I do not have a favorite book of all time, but a recent favorite is Girl, Wash Your Face by Rachel Hollis. It is a very relatable book that reminds you to stop doubting **yourself.**

Favorite quote?

"Life's challenges are not supposed to paralyze you, but help you discover who you are" by Bernice Johnson Reagon.

Best piece of business advice you ever received?

What other people think of you is none of your business.

Angela Cody, CEO Major Mom
Veteran, Major USAF

Best childhood memories.

My best childhood memories are visiting my grandparents at their farm in Indiana.

I would go there for Christmas each year with my mom and sister, and we would spend a week there in the summer. It was magical! Our grandparents gave us so much trust and responsibility at a very young age. I was allowed to collect eggs from the chickens without supervision, ride the huge lawn mower and cut the grass as well as, be around the horses, cows, and pigs. We were taught how to pick green beans and make incredible soups that my grandfather called Milly Mush. I did not eat it, but it sure was fun making it with grandpa. My grandfather and grandmother were amazing storytellers. They treated me with respect and kindness and taught me so much about life.

My grandmother has a saying, "Everything always works out for the best." My grandfather said, "That's bull*&%#." And then he would do something about it—he was very creative. He was fired a lot from his Speech Pathologist jobs so he would find another job and finally he just decided to do what he loved, art. He was an eccentric artist. He painted, made fabulous metal creations and mostly his livelihood and passion were that of a stone sculptor. He branded his work "The Touchables" and they are well-known throughout Indiana. I heard a pastor once say that "a child who winds up doing well has had at least one stable and committed relationship with a supportive adult." I am one of the lucky ones to have had two very supportive and stable grandparents for 48 years.

What were your favorite games to play growing up? Do any of those relate to who you are or what you do today?

I had two favorite games as a child in elementary school: Tether Ball and Red Rover. I had a fierce, competitive spirit like my grandparents, uncles, and mom. I liked Tether Ball because it was all about me. There was some strategy in Tether Ball, but it was mainly brute force and physics. If I lost, it was directly related to my abilities, even when the other person was clearly cheating. Playing with so many sore losers and cheaters made me more determined to win. The result was giving each game my all and the results were that I had fun most of the time, got hurt sometimes, and got in screaming matches with bullies. Red Rover was a game of strategy to me. I was so good at finding the weak link in the others teams' human hand-holding chain. I was always a leader on my team. From instructing the "weak links" to reinforcing the chain by arm holding instead of just holding by the hands but do it at the last second so our opponent could not break through our human chain and therefore we would add another link to our growing chain. The dedication and grit to win resulted in wins, losses, and bruises. Each loss made me stronger.

From the movie "Fallen", can you define what moment this was for you?

I have two Fallen Moments. The first was the moment when I tried to tell my mom that my stepfather was inappropriately reaching up my nightgown when we were playing and she said, "Well don't wear a nightgown." Or "Well then don't play with him while in a nightgown." That is what I heard. My mom was stoned and so was my stepfather. At age seven, I knew I was on my own to figure things out. My mom does not remember this event and there is no way I can prove this is how it went down, but it is exactly how I remember it. I held onto that story and the secret until I was 19.

My second Fallen Moment is when I came home for Christmas to visit my mom and she was still kind of with my stepdad (he rarely came home). I had an immense sense of guilt for leaving my sister in that mess. So, I told my mom that Fred molested me as a little girl, showed his privates, leered at me, intimidated me, threatened me, and verbally abused me. I also listed all the lies he had told her about me that I got in lots of trouble for. My mom was in shock. She said she believed me, and the next day on her way home to Bloomington from work in Indianapolis, she stopped at my grandfather's farm and told him what I had told her. She was afraid to go home because she was sure she would try to kill him and may end up getting killed herself. (We did not own guns.) My grandfather told my mom to stay at his house told her he was going to drive to Bloomington and tell him to leave. I learned that timing is everything:

i. My mom was finally ready to hear my cry for help

ii. My stepdad had no reason to stay with no kids in the house

iii. My grandfather became my hero

Memorable moment/event as a child:

One time, my mom and I jointly owned a house and several acres in Deland, Florida with my grandfather. My grandfather was a sculptor, and he liked doing art shows in Florida in the winter to get out of the Indiana cold. He had a workshop on the property, and we had chickens and pets. One day the police came to our house and looked for Fred. They said he had stolen a car, and someone reported seeing it at our house. My mom said she had no idea who they were looking for and had not seen the car. That day when we got home from school on the bus, she handed us big black trash bags and said, "We are moving to The Farm (our grandpa's house) tonight. Put whatever you want to take in these bags and put them in the car." We moved a lot, but this was when I had to get real about what was a treasure to me and what could be easily left behind. I got really good at leaving stuff behind, because also learned we would get more stuff at the next place.

Philosophical/spiritual underpinnings:

I gave my heart to Jesus at age seven. I was desperate for love and I did find wonderful peace via the bus ministry for Trinity Baptist Church in Clearwater, FL. I learned about a heavenly father that loved me when my earthly fathers had never displayed a love that I was receptive to.

Family structure, background, and experience:

My mom married my dad at age 19. She had me when she was 20, and my sister was born 18 months later. My dad was very abusive to my mother. She tried to leave him many times, but he would cry and beg her not to leave. I cared for my sister and myself at a very young age on numerous occasions because my dad was passed out drunk while my mom was working. She was such a hard worker. Through it all, she maintained an incredible sense of humor and grit. I could tell she loved my sister and me.

She told me many times, "All I ever wanted was to be a mom." She finally was able to resist getting back together with my dad when I was around five years old, and so he married another woman and left us in Florida. He moved to New York with her and started another family. My dad called us a few times the first year, and then we did not hear from him for many years. We would see him once every eight to 10 years for short and supervised visits at my mom's best friend's house in Indiana. My mom eventually went to school and became a nurse. She was a single mom, and she was exhausted, which led to her next bad choice of men: my stepfather. Fred, an escaped convict and chronic car thief as well as someone with the inability to keep his hands off my sister and me. My mom worked a lot, and she began working nights as a nurse because the pay was better at night and my stepdad could not work because he was "in hiding." He did offender-friendly jobs like construction where they pay you in cash. My mom never got to be a stay-at-home mom; she worked hard as a nurse for 35 years. We moved 16 times by the time I was 14, and some of those moves were out-of-state moves. It was a long, tough childhood sprinkled with hundreds of fabulous moments with my grandparents, friends, and other family members.

Educational and work experiences. What jobs or experiences contributed the most to your success? Why?

I began getting paid babysitting jobs in Houston, TX at the age of 12. This was an immense responsibility, and I took it seriously. I always prepared proper meals and cleaned up the house before the parents got home. I was incredibly responsible from a very young age. I began working at age 17 via the Office Education Association program at Bloomington High School South in Bloomington, IN. I was a receptionist at the Monroe County Public Library on Saturdays and Sundays and two evenings per week. I answered all incoming calls and transferred them to the correct departments within the library. I also had many administrative responsibilities to do between phone calls. I would help create the monthly newsletter and print out hundreds of copies via a huge ink rolling drum. They trusted me with much responsibility, and I loved it. I had lots of autonomy on the evening shifts and weekends because the other office staff was rarely in—they were the M-F 9am-5pm staff. The job that pushed me to the brink of insanity but also prepared me the most for entrepreneurship was my job in the United States Air Force as a Missile Combat Crew Commander. I had the keys to the nukes! Talk about constant training and a culture that accepted nothing less than perfect.

If your career could be told in a story, what would be the conflict, climax, and the antagonist, and what do you project to be a happy ending?

CONFLICT: Inability to be a good follower, always wanting to be the leader as an Air Force Officer.

CLIMAX: Resigned my commission in the USAF to be a stay-at-home mom and raise my kids and then the economy went into a Great Recession. We lost our real estate appraisal business and I had to go back to the drawing board.

ANTAGONIST: My creative passion for organizing. Robert Kiyosaki helped to create a burning desire to be a business owner.

HAPPY ENDING: Sell Major Organizers in 20 years for $10 million. Maintain my personal brand as Major Mom and speak/teach and inspire women and children to rise above the trenches and push forward no matter what.

If someone else were to tell your accomplishments, what would they say? What would the list entail?

Ha! They would say, "She is an over-achiever. She never stops. She does too much. I don't know how she does it all." My mom says, "You're a stud." That is a huge compliment and a reference to when my brother and I were rocking it together in an MLM company, Primerica Financial Services, as our side gig.

What did you do differently from colleagues to get to where you are?

I showed up to every meeting. I pursued professional development and got my MBA. I pushed myself hard. I had a reason to never want to repeat the first part of my life, my childhood. I also volunteered for every special assignment or project. I loved learning new things and building my skill set. It was a passion or obsession… maybe both. I wanted something more, I just did not know it was entrepreneurship.

Who or what has been your greatest inspiration?

I come from a very long line of women with grit. My mom works harder than any woman I know. She is a doer. My maternal great-grandmother immigrated to America from Germany for a better way of life. She could barely speak English. My maternal grandmother became a doctor after having five children. She left my grandfather and went on to have an incredible life, all while being the most supporting, loving, and generous parent and grandparent to her family. My grandmother helped ensure that I never made a man my plan. She was incredibly talented, smart, and athletic. My mother and I played tennis and golf together many times. She ensured I pursued higher education and she introduced me to investing in the stock market. One thing she used to say to me was, "Angie, I like you and I love you." I began to understand that you can love people you do not like, mainly out of familial obligations, but she took those obligations seriously.

What does "grit" mean to you?

Grit means to stop and lick your wounds and get back up! Keep on keepin' on. Onward and upward. Your dreams don't have to end at each failure. The path to your dreams just gets altered and the timeline gets extended, which stinks. Never give up. God does not put dreams in your heart, abilities in your soul, and talents in your hands to waste them by playing it safe.

What characteristics of grit do you have?

Courage MOST, being the new girl in 10 different schools and 13 years in the military took my natural courage to new heights. Conscientiousness. Achievement Oriented vs. Dependable. Very much achievement oriented.

Dependable. We have three families that wanted me to raise their kids in the event of their untimely passing. Follow Through. Long-term goals and endurance LEAST, I am not a details person. I am a visionary, so follow through on details is my weakest characteristic. When I hit a rough patch, I throttle back and regroup.

Resilience. optimism, confidence, and creativity most. Excellence vs. Perfection. Excellence. I am not a perfectionist. I am a good enough for now type of person.

How long or how many experiences did it take to ascertain this characteristic of grit/grittiness?

Hundreds of "iron sharpening iron" moments were not seen as a gift from God until I was around 45 years old! I am 48 now. My very long resume and list of achievements are the external proof of grit, but what you cannot see is my unwavering faith that God has plans for me greater than I have even allowed myself to believe. Hundreds of opportunities have presented themselves to me to try to get me to quit and play small. From my dad leaving, abuse from my stepfather, heart breaks from boys, being passed up for promotions or opportunities, sexually harassed in college and the USAF, victim of vicious rumors that greatly affected my reputation in my circle of influence, betrayal by a best friend, failing of an important career exam, divorce, several unsuccessful businesses and business attempts. I am exhausted just thinking of all my failures, but each one was a wakeup call that I was not on the right path. Having a squatter on my commercial property that required me to go to court to get her off, forced in to personal bankruptcy by a second lienholder on a rental that got foreclosed on and a rental that was short sold--during the Great Recession when we were heavily leveraged in residential rentals and a commercial real estate development project business partner squabbles, sued by a woman to whom I donated my organizing services for throwing away a 17th century chandelier and antique Care Bears (I won), lawsuit from a potential new hire in Arizona that I decided not to fight and gave her $25,000 for what my lawyer said was just another frivolous lawsuit, employees stealing clients and poaching my team, a total of 36 moves to date, most unwanted and burdensome, not taking a paycheck after 12 years in business as a reinvestment into franchising efforts and covering hard costs and this list goes on and on. True grit does not happen overnight. I have prayed many times, "Lord please! Give me a break here." However, I know He is preparing me for the rigors of having a national business. My pride was chipped away at like a diamond in the rough. My humility and wisdom were sharpened like iron sharpens iron. It takes a lot of heat to sharpen iron, but the results are measurable. The haters come out of the woodwork and the enemy of my soul shows up, but I fear no evil. I just keep pressing towards the mark.

What are your grittiest moments to date?

Getting a home organizing business off the ground during the Great Recession while downsizing three times to smaller and smaller homes and apartments.

I started my career as a Professional Home Organizer and was making very little money when I decided to build a company that could further my career and passions. I reinvested every penny I made organizing to creating a brand, hiring employees, and building a client base. I went without a paycheck from Major Mom Organizers for two years! My bookkeeper, Lisa, kept saying, "You need to pay yourself." I said, "I will. Someday I will." Building a national brand is a long game, not a short game. I waited tables at the Grand Lux Café in order to put food on the table for my family while I built my organizing business. I also was the project manager for our commercial development project during this time. During this time, my husband and I decided that we would continue to tithe 10% to our non-denominational church. It was important to always give to others even when we were so broke. We realized others do have it worse, and we must recognize our blessings.

What has been your greatest winning accomplishment so far?

My performance on the military episode of Shark Tank on Feb 5, 2016. I did not get a deal, but I showed true grit when I ended with my statement, "Onward and upward. I will create a national brand."

Mentorship vs. Sponsorship –what is the difference?

A mentor invests in you for no personal gain or with no expectations of tit for tat. A sponsor expects something in return for their time and/ or money.

Did/do you have a sponsor, coach, or mentor? If so, what do you believe is the most valuable information you have gleaned or help you were given?

I have had many mentors, sponsors, and coaches. Anyone with true grit knows you do not climb up any wall by yourself. The most valuable information I gleaned from all of them could only come from someone with outside perspective. It is impossible to see what others can see because you are too close and intimidate with all the details of your career/life/business. I rebranded my company twice thanks to a few mentors. In 2006, my home organizing company was called Organized 4 Life, LLC. In 2008, I rebranded to Major Mom. I was a Major in the Air Force when I became a mom, and that was the nickname my husband gave me. Then, after appearing on Shark Tank and listening to not only the Sharks; Aaron Kennedy, founder of Noodles & Company; and Mary a franchisor and a couple other women with grit, I rebranded to Major Organizers for the company and kept Major Mom as my personal brand that I speak and teach under.

How did you find your sponsor, coach, or mentor?

When the student is ready, the teacher appears. When I was ready and knew I needed help, I found it.

Who has contributed or what has contributed to your success more than anything?

The following books profoundly affected me for the good: Built to Last; Rich Dad, Poor Dad; Think and Grow Rich, Millionaire Mind, How to Win Friends and Influence People and E-Myth. The greatest tipping point for me to begin a career and business as a professional organizer was attending T. Harv Eker's free Millionaire Mind Intensive in Denver, Colorado. I immediately joined a mastermind group with other attendees there. I was in a mastermind group for three years, and it changed my way of thinking forever.

"I want every one of you to become the subject of someone else's story of overcoming." What does this mean to you?

It means that each step of the way towards your dreams, don't forget to look back and help someone along their path to their dreams. I have mentored many veterans and civilian women. I have also been an accountability partner to six different entrepreneurs.

What are some words of wisdom and no-nonsense advice you have received?

My husband and I realized the need to shut down our residential real estate business with $30,000 in aged receivables, could not find jobs, and were downsizing into an apartment. I was doing one fix and flip at a time. One day, my husband came home, and I was watching my favorite show with my little ones, "Clean Sweep." It was a show that featured Peter Walsh, and he cleared out several rooms in homes and organized them. I loved that show and the whole process. My husband said, "Angela, you should be doing that for a living. You love organizing and you do it for everyone you know." I thought that was such a dumb thing to say. I had never met a professional organizer outside of Oprah and home improvement shows. Well, that was 12 years ago, and it was incredible wisdom and advice.

What is the greatest difference between you and your male counterpart, if any?

There are very few male counterparts in the home organizing world. However, it does seem from my viewpoint that many of the successful men in the industry have no children or are empty nesters. So, they are able to spend the 60-80 hours required to build their businesses faster than I am able to at this season of my motherhood.

If you had to do something all over again, good or bad, what would it be?

Ha! My son's friends would say "do-over" when they did not like the results of the game they were currently playing. I remember feeling very agitated, so I said, "No, there are no do overs. If you did not get a good push off the wall, you keep swimming to you get to the other end and still try to win the race. You do not scream 'do-over.' There are no do-overs!" Do-overs are not real, and they are not an option. The only option is to learn from the moments where you wished you would have done something differently, but also to accept that maybe things worked out the way they were supposed to.

Can you describe the uniqueness of your role or a career relative to women?

I landed in a career as a residential professional organizer. The productivity and organizing industry are 90% female. That presents many CEO opportunities. Currently, according to the National Association of Productivity and Organizing (NAPO), 78% of home organizing companies are solopreneurs. Many of these solopreneurs subcontract each other to get larger jobs done. This is awesome, because it shows the natural cooperative nature of women and our ability to be cooperative versus competitive. In this industry, we have the opportunity to be the CEO and an executive. We also have the burdensome responsibility to figure out how to grow large enough to be considered a CEO by the world's standards.

If we are to make strides towards Fortune's goal of 100X25, we must...

Have mentors and investors come to our industry that have built multi-million-dollar service businesses and show us the way. There is something I do not know. A nugget that will help me figure out why I got stuck at the $500,000 mark and seemed to have regressed in revenues as I expand. We must be shown the way. Some things are not intuitive, and some roadblocks and potholes must be navigated around. Many women just keep hitting the roadblocks and potholes, and we cannot figure out a way around them by ourselves. As an economy, we must continue to find, identify, and reach out to women with vast potential and pull them up one of the rungs. Many of us get stuck and need someone either to kick us in the buns or get us unstuck or give us a hand-up, not a handout. That hand up may be capital, it may be a job, or it may be mentorship and coaching.

Is this possible in your industry...why?

Yes, we are 75% female, so it better be. However, we have so far to go. To date, we do not have a home organizing business that has created a millionaire. The industry needs a few leaders to pull up its status from a cutesy hobby that a stay-at-home mom does to legitimate career that a woman with an education thrives in. This is why I felt led to franchise. I feel called to help elevate the industry's status amongst the big boys and girls.

Essential daily or weekly reads?

The Bible every day. I wish I could say that I have read the Bible from front to back, but I have not. I got into the habit of just reading devotionals and little snippets from the Bible. However, at our church in California, the whole church reads the Bible in a year, and it is the best kind of peer pressure peer pressure to do the right thing. I had no idea how much God's word would soften my heart towards my husband and other people in my life that are really hard to deal with appropriately.

What do women need to do more of to reach the highest levels in corporate America or beyond?

I think our Creator designed all humans to have feminine and masculine traits. Our cultures determine that males will display more masculine traits and women should display more feminine traits. With that said, being authentic to your inner gifts and wisdom will help women get ahead. If women keep allowing themselves to be influenced to "lead like a man," it takes away the incredible feminine qualities that are necessary to be at the top. I do not mean women should cry at meetings, but I do mean to have mercy and grace with people as well as build them up, not tear them down.

What do women need to do less of to reach the highest levels or corporate America?

Women need to stop using their bodies and sexuality to get to the top. In other words, cover up the cleavage and lengthen the skirts, ladies. We do not need to look sexy at work to get noticed. We need to look professional. I love pant suits, and I was thankful in the United States Air Force that I had the option to wear the skirt or the pants, and I rarely chose the skirt. I wanted to blend in with my male counterparts as much as possible. A strong female mentor in the workplace and a good male mentor with the courage to say, "Cover it up at work" are essential to evening out the playing field. Goodness do not read this the wrong way. No one deserves sexual harassment. Modesty is the best policy in any work environment. I personally am tired of seeing bra straps, underlines, and belly buttons in the workplace—it is so distracting. This was not an issue in the military, but it is rampant in Corporate America.

Favorite movie of all time and why?

Beaches. It shows that women can have longevity of friendship even through fights over men, differences in upbringing and heated discussions that result in hurt feelings. They seemed to always forgive each other, and, in the end, their friendship became the cornerstone for the next generation. Having a true best friend brings so much comfort. It is so nice to not have to be guarded and timid around your bestie. It is so rare to be accepted for all your faults. I just love this movie so much.

Favorite book of all time and why?

The Bible. You can read a passage repeatedly, and it speaks to you in different ways as you mature. It is written in the most brilliant format. Even if you do not believe in God, reading it has tons of lessons on leadership, family, relationships, communities, having a vision, having a purpose, and most importantly, the grace, mercy, and forgiveness necessary to press on. I hope to finally finish The Bible this year. I have avoided reading it for a long time. Bummer, because it could have helped me not feel so anxious and worried about my past, present, and future.

Favorite quote?

Pastor Timothy Bagwell, from Word of Life Christian Center: “You are who God says you are!” I love this quote because many people will tell you to stop dreaming or that you don’t have the right connections, or you just don’t have any talent or beauty. The Pastor helped me realize something very profound.

When I am not working, I am:

Hanging out with my kids by taking road trips, going out to eat, and traveling abroad.

It is essential for women to know _____ and do _____:

It is essential for women to know how to listen to their gut and do what it is telling them to do.

When I was at a low point, even my lowest point, it was important that I do _____to survive:

Sleep! Sometimes getting to sleep required a glass or two of wine or a cup of SleepyTime Tea or an all-natural sleep aid, but sleeping is the one form of self-care I tend to implement more frequently than exercise.

If I could redo/relive a professional moment, it would be:

There are so many professional moments I would do over again! Each moment I made mistakes, I learned valuable lessons. However, I made the choice not to attend our company Christmas party because I lived in another state at the time and had kids and responsibilities. The decision sent the wrong signal to my team. As a mother, wife, career woman, and church volunteer, they are many times when my loyalties feel divided. I do not always make the right decision about where to spend my time.

People would be surprised if they knew I:

Was a cheerleader in elementary school, a wrestlerette sophomore year of high school, and participated in a scholarship beauty pageant senior year.

Best piece of business advice I ever received came from _______ and was_____:

Many different authors and coaching programs have all said the same thing: "Surround yourself with people smarter than you at all times."

Jeri Royce, President & CEO

Esperanca

Jeri Royce is the President and CEO of the Phoenix based, global organization Esperanca. Esperanca works locally and globally to improve health and provide hope through disease prevention, education and treatment for every life we touch.

Jeri is an accomplished leader with a distinguished career leading operational, business development, program development/ management and human resource functions. With over 25 years of experience in local and national nonprofit organizations, she has a successful track record of building a leading strong partnerships and highly successful teams. Having founded her own consulting firm, 3P-Leadership. She is a capacity-building consultant in the Virginia Piper Trust ATLAS and Good Governance programs. Jeri has previously served as Interim ED for Lead for Good, Arizona Public Health Association and Arizona Asthma Coalition.

Philosophical/spiritual underpinnings:

Being of service is more important than getting or having money, success, fame, etc. When your focus is to be of service the rest follows.

Your Greatest Inspiration?

I have to say my Mom. She is the grittiest person I know. She has faced and overcome adversities her entire life. She is strong, loving and compassionate and never complains.

What does "grit" mean to you?

For me grit is having the strength within that enables me stand strong and be courageous in the face of adversity.

What characteristics of grit do you have?

Strength, self-confidence, perseverance, resolve, tenacity.

How long or how many experiences did it take to ascertain this characteristic of grit/grittiness?

It feels like a lifetime. While I always exhibited grit, even as a young girl, I feel more settled in that part of myself because of the experiences I've faced in my life.

What are your grittiest moments to date?

My grittiest moment by far was being diagnosed with breast cancer in 2017. Begin able to keep moving forward in the face of such fear was difficult. My family and my strong spiritual foundation are what got me through.

Mentorship vs. Sponsorship –what is the difference?

I think of mentorship as guiding someone through your experience while sponsorship is a more direct form of support.

Did/do you have a sponsor, coach, or mentor? If so, what do you believe is the most valuable information you have gleaned or help you were given?

I had a mentor when I worked for a national nonprofit in DC. He taught me the importance of balancing my decision-making between emotion and logic at a time when women were encouraged to ignore their emotions. And he once said to me "Jeri, you can never be a great leader if you are afraid of losing your job." I was shocked at the time but have come to realize how incredibly right he was. As long as self-preservation is a motivation, our leadership can be misguided or withheld. We see it in politics every day – politicians are so busy trying to keep their jobs, they forget to do their jobs and lead on behalf of those they represent.

How did you find your sponsor, coach, or mentor?

He was my boss at the time, and we have remained friends.

Who has contributed or what has contributed to your success more than anything?

Staying connected to my heart while using my strong intellect.

If you had to do something all over again, good or bad, what would it be?

I was building my career while I was also raising children. At that time, having children had to come second to your job or career. If it didn't, you weren't taken seriously and didn't get promoted. I missed things in both my children's lives – school plays, sports events, being homeroom mom – that I wish I hadn't.

Favorite quote?

"What I know for sure is that every day brings a chance for you to draw in a breath, kick off your shoes, and step out and dance – to live free of regret and filled with as much joy, fun, and laughter as you can stand. You can either waltz boldly onto the stage of life and live the way you know your spirit is nudging you to, or you can sit quietly by the wall, receding into the shadows of ear and self-doubt." Oprah Winfrey

People would be surprised if they knew I was:

I am an avid fly fisherman (or should that be fisherwoman? 😊)

Best piece of business advice I ever received:

The best piece of advice I ever received came from colleague and friend. Her advice was to stop striving for work-life balance – it does not exist. Instead strive for work-life integration which makes room for both my professional life and personal life at the same time– not in equal parts but proportionate to what's needed at the time.

Joanna Dodd Massey, Ph.D.

President & CEO, J.D. Massey Associates, Inc.

Best childhood memories.

Christmastime. My father was compulsive about our tree. He would saw off branches and rewire them so that the tree made a perfect triangle. At the time, I would roll my eyes. "Why can't I just hang the ornaments?!" Which is why I now have a fake tree. It's much easier to manipulate the position of the branches when they're already wired to the frame.

Favorite games to play growing up? Do any of those relate to who you are or what you do today?

I watched a lot of TV. At one point, my pediatrician told my mother that it was excessive and not good for me. I subsequently spent more than 25 years as an executive in the television and film industries.

Educational and work experiences. What jobs or experiences contributed the most to your success? Why?

At 32 years old, I was named Senior Vice President of Media Relations for UPN, one of only six broadcast TV networks in the United States. It was a big career jump and a job that I loved.

If someone else were to tell your accomplishments, what would they say? What would the list entail?

I will tell you what they DO say—to me! "Would you stop already? You have so many graduate degrees that there are more letters after your name than in your name." My friends think I am a workaholic. They also say that I have a lot of impressive accomplishments, too numerous to name, but my biggest strength is my ability to pivot. I am the Queen of Pivoting.

What did you do differently from colleagues to get to where you are?

I embrace change and am constantly pivoting. When someone tells me, "No," I find a different way to get it done.

Who or what has been your greatest inspiration?

My mom. She was a stockbroker on Wall Street for more than 50 years and did not retire until age 77. She says, when life is tough, just put on your blinders and plod ahead.

What does "grit" mean to you?

Fortitude—having courage, strength and resilience. Remember, I am the Queen of Pivoting. That is not an easy title to hold, because it's a rollercoaster ride.

What characteristics of grit do you have?

(I think my answer to the question above also answers this one. Maybe it would be better put here.)

How long or how many experiences did it take to ascertain this characteristic of grit/grittiness?

On the final weekend of my Executive MBA program at the University of Southern California (USC) in 2016, we had a group session with a business coach who had us all pick a word that best describes us. I don't remember what word I picked, but one of my classmates picked "grit." A few weeks later, I was flipping through my photos from graduation and I noticed that the commencement speaker had a big screen behind him with an image of the word GRIT typed in all caps. I texted it to her and, ever since then, we check in with each other every few months to ask, "How is grit going?"

What has been your greatest winning accomplishment so far?

Making it this far in life... Seriously, life is hard. I try to remind myself to enjoy the rollercoaster ride, because I can't remember 99.9% of the things that freaked me out 20 years ago, but I sure as heck know that 20 years went by quickly. Four graduate degrees gave me a lot of knowledge, but it takes wisdom to know that the beauty of life is in both the ups and the downs.

Mentorship vs. Sponsorship –what is the difference?

A mentor is someone who picks up the phone. A sponsor is someone who opens doors.

Did/do you have a sponsor, coach, or mentor? If so, what do you believe is the most valuable information you have gleaned or help you were given?

I have had many mentors. My favorite piece of advice came from Dawn Ostroff, who was my boss at three different companies. She used to say to me, "Joanna, always ask the question. The worst they can say is no."

Who has contributed or what has contributed to your success more than anything?

Luck. People hate when I say that. They want to believe they had something to do with their success, but they don't. It's all luck. I learned that as a model when I was 5 years old and I was discovered while in a playground in Central Park. Going to acting and modeling auditions throughout childhood, I discovered that I could knock the ball out of the park during an audition, but if they were looking for red hair and green eyes, I was not getting the job as a blond with brown eyes. My whole career has come down to being in the right place at the right time to land the perfect job. Even pivoting is about luck. I was downsized right before the 2008 Recession, so I went back to school and got a Ph.D. in psychology. Right before graduation, I decided I wanted to go back to working as an executive in Hollywood. I made a few phone calls and eight weeks later, I had two job offers. I couldn't have planned that timing or that kind of good fortune. It was luck. If you're spiritual, then you will say it was God (or whatever word you use for a higher power).

What is the greatest difference between you and your male counterpart, if any?

I make at least $100,000 less (at least!).

If we are to make strides towards Fortune's goal of 100X25, we must...

Take a chance and think outside the box. A very smart woman, who ran PR at CBS in the 1990s, thought out of the box and took a chance when she hired me. She could have hired any number of people from inside the entertainment industry. At the time, I was working at a PR firm in technology and she wanted someone with a totally different perspective. It didn't matter that I didn't know the ins and outs of the job. She knew I was smart, and I would figure it out.

Is this possible in your industry...why?

It is absolutely possible in the media industry. We have innumerable smart, capable, seasoned female executives who are getting elevated to higher positions. The biggest problem is that Hollywood is still an old boys club—from the Board room to the C-Suite, most of these women have male bosses, so it is going to take a "woke" male to look beyond his implicit bias (and possibly explicit bias) and hire a woman.

Essential daily or weekly reads?

I glance at 165 e-news alerts a day (I know it is at least 165, because on those days when I can't read them all day long, my newsletter inbox always reads 165). As a communications executive, I have to know what the press are reporting on and what they're saying about it.

What do women need to do more of to reach the highest levels in corporate America or beyond?

If you asked me this 20 years ago, I would have said women need to act more like men in order to get ahead in business. Today, I think the opposite. Being a woman is our superpower and we need to use it.

Favorite movie of all time and why?

"Airplane"

Striker: "Surely, you can't be serious."

Rumack: "I am serious… and don't call me Shirley."

I love popcorn movies! (That's a term for a movie that doesn't have a lot of intellectual depth; it's just broad entertainment.)

Favorite book of all time and why?

"The Four Agreements" by Dom Miguel Ruiz. It's one of those books that led to a huge perception shift.

Favorite quote?

Anaïs Nin said that human beings can handle absolutely anything in the moment.

When I say it to people, I add my own twist on it by saying, "Human beings can handle absolutely anything in the moment… It's the thinking about it that causes the problems."

Keep my head in the same room as my feet.

Sharon Preszler, Captain Southwest Airlines
Lieutenant Colonel, Air Force (Retired)

Best childhood memories.

We didn't have much money growing up. My mom and dad divorced when I was six or seven, so most of the fun things we did were free. I loved going to the beaches in Southern California and body surfing and driving up into the San Bernardino mountains for snowball fights and sledding in the winter and rock climbing in the summer. When I was 5, we flew from England to Los Angeles (we had gone to live with my mom's parents while my dad served in Thailand during the Vietnam war). It is the first flight I actually remember, and it was amazing! I loved everything about flying - looking at the clouds from above, helping the stewardesses pass out snacks, the feeling of freedom that comes from not being earthbound. But the best part was when we were crossing the Atlantic Ocean and the stewardesses took my sister and me up to the cockpit. It was nighttime, and the sky was so black you could see what seemed like a billion stars. Looking at the white swath the Milky Way was making across the night sky took my breath away. When I went back to my seat, I told my mom

I wanted to be a stewardess when I grew up. My mom, who was very forward-thinking for 1970, asked if I wouldn't rather be a pilot. I realized that the pilots got to stare at that beautiful sky all the time, and my mind was made up. From then on, I knew I wanted to be a pilot.

What were your favorite games to play growing up? Do any of those relate to who you are or what you do today?

My favorite games to play growing up were sports. I loved baseball and volleyball and played basketball. I think playing team sports had a huge impact on who I am today. Learning to be part of a team when you are young has so may valuable lessons for "regular" jobs in adult life; putting the needs of the team before your own, helping others get better so your team will be better, realizing that being a great player doesn't make you a great leader, accomplishing goals (winning) takes hard work, seeing lots of different coaching styles and thinking about what type of leader you want to be, realizing you may have to adapt your style to that of your team, healthy competition brings out the best in us, and teammates will respect your performance regardless of your background. As I look back on the very non-traditional life I have lived to this point, I know that being the only girl in my little league in the late '70s taught me so many things I needed later in life.

From the movie Fallen, can you define what moment this was for you?

It may be unusual, but I have two life-changing moments. The first came when I was selected to be the first woman in the Air Force to fly the F-16. I was 28 years old, one year out of pilot training, married to my incredibly supportive husband of eight years, and standing at a press conference with General McPeak, the Chief of Staff of the Air Force, and two other women pilots, Jeannie Flynn and Martha Mc Sally. Gen McPeak was explaining to the press how the combat exclusion for women had been overturned by Congress and that we were going to be the initial cadre of female fighter pilots in the USAF. As I was answering questions from the press, everything became real to me. I had started down a path that I never dreamed would be open to me and it was exciting and terrifying at the same time. I couldn't wait to start training in the F-16, but I also knew that women fighter pilots were a very unpopular idea in parts of the fighter community - the very community I would work so hard to become a part of.

The second life altering moment came after I was an established F-16 instructor pilot and well respected in the fighter community. I was 38 years old, had been in the Air Force for 17 years, and aspired to be an F-16 Squadron Commander. James and I had a beautiful two-year-old boy with wispy blonde hair and a permanent smile on his face. We had just moved to Sumter, South Carolina, and I was settling into my new squadron and learning a new mission in the F-16. While traveling to Oklahoma for my brother's wedding, our son Collin started running a mild fever and was a little lethargic. It got worse overnight and we took him to an acute care clinic. They did some blood work and told us to rush him to the Children's hospital. While we were waiting to be seen by the doctor, Collin's lips started turning blue. James went and got a nurse and they put him on oxygen, and he started looking better. When the doctor finally came into the room she asked if we knew what they thought was wrong with Collin. When we said no, she bluntly told us they thought he had cancer. At that moment, my entire world shattered. I felt like I was going to be physically sick. I handed Collin to James and went out into the hallway to settle myself down because I didn't want to scare Collin. It turned out, Collin had a highly treatable form of Leukemia and responded very well to his three years of treatment. Today he is a strong, healthy young man who still smiles a lot, and we are incredibly thankful for the doctors and nurses who became such a big part of our daily lives. Collin's illness changed my primary focus from career to family. I retired from the Air Force a few years later without ever getting the opportunity to be a Squadron Commander, but it didn't matter to me anymore. My family was stronger than ever, and my son was healthy.

What jobs or experiences contributed the most to your success? Why?

I have a BS in Computer Science and Math and an MS in Aerospace Studies. I needed a college degree to be an officer in the Air Force and the college experience was good for me, but I never really used my degree. I think it was undergraduate pilot training that contributed the most to my success. It is an intense year of training that not only teaches you to fly but also teaches you to be calm under pressure and handle emergencies without panicking. I was also the class leader and the opportunity to hold together a group of 20 young people who were competing with each other, not just to graduate but to do well enough to get the airplane of their choice, taught me a lot about leadership I was able to use later.

If your career could be told in a story, what would be the conflict, climax, and the antagonist, and what do you project to be a happy ending?

The conflict would definitely be integrating women into fighters. The antagonists would be fighter pilots who fought against the change - openly and covertly. The climax would be when I felt comfortable in my squadron and my squadron mates actively defended me to others. The happy ending will be in about 11 years, when I retire from commercial aviation, and I have maintained my good reputation, effectively mentored those who have come behind me, and a new woman pilot joining a squadron is just a new pilot, not a new woman pilot.

If someone else were to tell about your accomplishments, what would they say? What would the list entail?

First woman to fly F-16s in the USAF, first woman in combat in the F-16, first woman instructor in the F-16, first woman Squadron Director of Operations (second in charge of a squadron) in the F-16, well respected F-16 instructor pilot, key player in the cultural transformation of USAF Fighter Squadrons as they integrated women, Captain at Southwest Airlines, mother to an amazing son, and wife to an incredible husband.

What did you do differently from colleagues to get to where you are?

I didn't do things differently as much as I was different. Because I was different and the first woman venturing into this particular man's world, I was forced to be an instrument of cultural transformation in the USAF fighter community. It was a lot of pressure knowing that you could never blend in or "fly under the radar." People were always watching me - some hoping I would succeed and some hoping I would fail. But, either way, I knew they were watching my progress. I also felt early on that the hopes of all women who would ever want to fly fighters rested on my shoulders. That is a lot to take on in an already intense and sometimes hostile training environment, and it took me a while to learn to deal with the additional pressure.

Who or what has been your greatest inspiration?

The Women Air Service Pilots or WASPs. The WASPs were created during World War II to ferry airplanes around the U.S. and the world to free male pilots up for combat missions. If you can, imagine women flying B-17s and P-51s in the '40s and the reception they would get. It was amazing to read their stories. I hadn't even heard about them until I finished pilot training, but I knew all their stories before I was selected to go fly fighters. Once I learned I would get to go fly F-16s and realized what that would entail, I was so happy to know there were women who went before me who faced similar obstacles and attitudes and were successful. I knew I owed it to them to do my absolute best to break one more barrier.

What does Grit mean to you?

There is little agreement on what grit truly is and if it something you are born with or develop over time through overcoming challenges. Not having enough grit can be used to explain away systemic discrimination or to justify promotion beyond someone's performance level. I can see how it is a heated topic.

Which characteristics do you possess the most of and the least of?

I think I have many characteristics in differing amounts. It definitely took courage and follow through to make it through F-16 training and then move with my husband to Germany to meet my new squadron, a squadron that I knew some of them didn't want me in. I have always been achievement oriented and resilient. I sometimes wonder if my resilience is really just stubbornness. I am generally optimistic and confident but feel I lack creativity- I'm just too determined or stubborn to give up on my goals. Excellence versus perfection has always been a struggle for me. It took a long time for me to realize perfection was most likely unattainable and if I focused on trying to be perfect at one thing, performance in all the other things in my life would suffer. Excellence versus perfection to me is a matter of prioritization and time management. I decided perfection in any aspect of my life (work, family, other interests) takes too much of my time and leaves no energy for the other things that are important to me. Perfection is definitely the enemy of good enough.

How long or how many experiences did it take to ascertain this characteristic of grit/grittiness?

I think our "grittiness" is always developing and changing. I can look back and see things from my childhood that toughened me up, but nothing that truly prepared me for what I faced as the Air Force's instrument of change. I think a lot of it comes from how you are raised. Do your parents encourage you to take risks? Are you raised to believe it is better to have tried and failed than never to try at all? Or are you raised in a sheltered and protected manner, so you never get hurt but you also aren't challenged and don't build that confidence or resiliency? I believe that, most of the time, you don't know what you can handle in terms of challenges until you are in the middle of them. Courage allows you to accept the challenge. Then, you use your prior experiences and those characteristics of resiliency and being achievement oriented and you focus on what you want to accomplish. To me, it was about choices. Am I going to let someone else tell me what I can or can't do? Am I going to prove them wrong? Am I going to make sure that if I fail, I have tried my absolute best?

What are your grittiest moments to date?

The press conference with General McPeak announcing that women would be allowed to fly fighters. It became real at that moment and I had truly put myself out there. There was no going back, and I knew I had a rough road ahead. Walking into my F-16 training squadron at Luke Air Force Base was another. I had no idea how I would be received by my classmates and my instructors. It's a lot easier to handle once you figure out who is supportive and who isn't, but I was walking in blind and didn't know a soul.

Moving to Germany to join my first operational F-16 Squadron was another tough moment. I would finally be a combat ready F-16 pilot, but it felt like starting all over again. I knew some of my squadron mates had already judged me and didn't want me there. Again, I didn't know anyone and was very unsure about how I would be received. It worked out in the long run, but it definitely took some grit to show up that first day. Going back to flying after my successful ejection from an F-16 at the end of the runway at Luke AFB due to brake failure. I never doubted I would fly the F-16 again, but when the time came, it took more courage than I expected to suit up and go fly. For the next few weeks, I wouldn't think about the ejection at all until I landed and went to step on the brakes. Then it would flicker through my brain, "I wonder if my brakes are going to work today?" They always did, but the thought went through my mind. Bringing our two-year-old son home from the hospital after his initial treatment for Leukemia. He had been in the hospital a little over a week and we were all ready to go home. But when we were home, we were responsible for giving him his medicine three times a day and monitoring him for any setbacks. We lost the safety net the nurses and doctors provided. That entire three years was full of gritty moments for us, but I still remember how scared I was to bring him home.

What has been your greatest winning accomplishment so far?

When I retired from the Air Force in 2006, I was a well-respected instructor in the F-16. I was accepted throughout the F-16 community as just another pilot, and I saw the women who came behind me being successful and being welcomed without all the trepidation that I faced. We are still a tiny minority of fighter pilots, but women are generally accepted. There are still battles being fought, but they are fewer and farther apart than 25 years ago.

Did/do you have a sponsor, coach, or mentor? If so, what do you believe is the most valuable information you have gleaned or help you were given?

No, not really.

Who has contributed or what has contributed to your success more than anything?

The support of my husband and family made the biggest difference for me. When things weren't going well, my husband, James, was always there for me, and I knew he would always be there for me regardless of whether I succeeded or failed. You can take on a lot of challenges when you have someone like that supporting you,

"I want every one of you to become the subject of someone else's story of overcoming." What does this mean to you?

I think we all have a responsibility to help those following in our footsteps. Being the first woman to fly the F-16 was tough in a lot of ways. If I don't actively help the next generation of woman fighter pilots, how is it going to be any easier for them?

What are some words of wisdom and no-nonsense advice you have received?

Growing up, my mom would always tell my sister and me that "Life's not fair." We both hated that advice at the time, but looking back, it really helped us. If you don't expect life to be fair, it is easier to handle when it isn't. If life were fair, integrating women into fighter squadrons would have been easy - it would have simply been about how well you fly the jet. Instead, it was about flying the jet and ego, personality, fear of change, fitting in, and squadron unity. It definitely was not fair, but I was ready for it.

What is the greatest difference between you and your male counterpart, if any?

As a woman fighter pilot, there was never any way to blend in. At one point, the Air Education and Training Commander, a General, was getting daily reports on my progress. While the daily reports ended, there was still a lot of attention. Every mistake I made and some of my successes were spread throughout the F-16 community.

If you had to do something all over again, good or bad, what would it be?

I would like to do F-16 initial training again. I learned so many valuable lessons about myself during those nine months that would make the emotional side of training (the pressure, the instructors, and my fellow students) so much easier and I would have more energy to just focus on my flying.

Can you describe the uniqueness of your role or a career relative to women?

Almost 25 years after I started in the F-16 and 12 years after I retired from the USAF, there are between 50 and 60 active women fighter pilots in the USAF. They are authorized over 3,700. So, women fighter pilots are about 1-2% of the fighter force. I guess you can say I am a one-percenter.

Essential daily or weekly reads

The Wall Street Journal and The BBC news. I cannot watch the [U.S.] news anymore. I do not read the financial news in the WSJ, but I think they have a good perspective on other news. I also like the BBC's perspective on our national news.

What do women need to do more of to reach the highest levels in corporate America or beyond?

We need to mentor and support each other more. Too often, we compete with each other instead of making each other better. Hopefully, we will realize that a successful woman is good for all of us.

What do women need to do less of to reach the highest levels or corporate America?

We need to realize it is virtually impossible to have it all, and unfortunately, if you want to get to the top, you probably need to spend less time away from work for your family. It takes sacrifice for anyone to reach the top so something will have to give. It would be nice if dads left work early for school field trip or soccer games, but it does not usually happen, and even when it does, it is viewed differently than when women do it. I think it is still asking too much to be a CEO (or on a CEO track) and a mom to younger children. Please remember, I am a mom who made this choice about 15 years ago. Things may have changed, but it was nearly impossible to have everything then.

Favorite movie of all times and why?

"A League of Their Own" (1992). It was a fun movie that showed women in non-traditional roles and demonstrated the different expectations of male coaches (or managers or supervisors) and women players (or team members or employees). I did not realize it at the time, but it was a metaphor for the challenge I would take on a few years later.

Favorite book of all time and why?

On Silver Wings: The Women Airforce Service Pilots of WWII. I had never heard of the WASPs until after I completed pilot training.

Once I heard about them, I found a few books about them and read their stories. They were amazing women, definitely full of grit, who flew every airplane in the Air Force industry, delivering them where they were needed. And that was in the '40s! They were so inspiring.

Favorite quote?

"Life is far too important to be taken seriously." ¾Oscar Wilde. I remind myself of this quote often, usually when I am taking things way too seriously. We need to make time for fun in our busy lives. Take time to play a game with your son or daughter, have lunch with friends, or dinner and a movie with your husband. You will be happier and healthier for it, and that will reflect in your work. Apparently, the actual quote is Life is far too important a thing ever to talk seriously about, but over time it was misquoted and shifted to the commonly known quote above.

When I am not working, I am:

Traveling, reading, scuba diving, skiing, or hanging out at home with my family (including my two dogs).

It is essential for women to know ______ and do _____:

It is important for women to know it is okay to put themselves first sometimes. As a working mom, I often feel torn between time spent at work and time spent caring for my family. If you let it, you can use all your time on work and family and not have any left for yourself. It is important to prioritize your needs sometimes - have a girl's night out, get a massage, soak in the tub, or read a book you have been putting off. In the long run, a happy and healthy mom is better for the family.

When I was at a low point, even my lowest point, it was important that I do _____to survive:

It was important that I focus on the people who care about me. I was having a hard time dealing with the pressure in F-16 training, and eventually I made my mantra the old saying "Those who matter don't mind and those who mind don't matter." I needed to remind myself that my husband and family supported me unconditionally, and all the people that were hoping I would fail did not matter to me. It takes a while to internalize the attitude this saying promotes, but if you can dismiss the naysayers and focus on those who love and support you, it is amazing what you can do!

When equating my life and success to a real person or fictitious character, I would choose:

I would choose the WASPs (Women Airforce Service Pilots). They broke gender barriers in aviation before I was even born and were an inspiration to me. I am proud to have been able to follow in their footsteps, and I like to think that if I were alive during WWII, I would have been a WASP.

People would be surprised if they knew I:

I hate the cold but like snow skiing! I will tolerate the cold for the freedom of the mountain.

Cheryl Levick, CEO

CLL Business Enterprises

Best childhood memories.

Cheryl grew up in St. Louis, in the Midwest, and was a middle child from a middle-income family. During her first 20 years, she wanted to do everything her older sister by 22 months (and only sibling) did. Idle hands were not considered positive, and she was made to get outside and do other things. Cheryl remembers being outside all the time. Her grandmother had a farm, and she would take the horses out each morning after her and Pam packed a lunch. Perhaps the beginning of teamwork was learned here. Stay together; "every fence you open, you close." She was also active in Girl Scouts and loved camping outdoors through junior high school. The summers would be spent playing softball, and during school she played any sport, even synchronized swimming.

What were your favorite games to play growing up? Do any of those relate to who you are or what you do today?

Cheryl played softball, engaged in water skiing, enjoyed sports, and was good at everything except golf. She loved academics and athletics.

From the movie "Fallen," can you define what moment this was for you?

Birth of each child; Getting married and divorced. The 1989 earthquake while at Stanford. As mentioned, she divorced her husband who later committed suicide while her daughter was a freshman at UCLA. She was already a dedicated mother, but now had to become a dedicated father. How did she do it? She mentioned having an incredible network and support system at Stanford.

What jobs or experiences contributed the most to your success? Why?

B.S., University of Missouri; M.S., Indiana University; 35 years hands-on athletic administration experience; 12 years as Director of Athletics at four Division I institutions; SportsBusiness Journal "Game Changer"; NACWAA D1 Athletic Administrator of the Year.

Cheryl also served as Senior Associate Director of Athletics at the University of Maryland (UM); Director of Athletics at Saint Louis University; and Director of Athletics at Santa Clara University. At each institution, she managed all day-to-day operations, budgets, fundraising, facilities, and capital projects.

Additionally, Cheryl spent 12 years as Senior Associate Athletics Director at Stanford University. There, Cheryl served as Deputy AD/COO of the athletic department, managed a $30 million budget, oversaw 33 varsity sports, won 42 National Championships, and supervised eight Olympic Coaches.

Cheryl's experience in national collegiate athletic administration also includes: Assistant Commissioner, Pac-10 (now Pac-12) Conference; National Collegiate Athletic Association (NCAA); Executive Program, Stanford Business School

If your career could be told in a story, what would be the conflict, climax, and the antagonist, and what do you project to be a happy ending?

Cheryl's childhood was in fact an indication of her future – she loved sports and loved learning. It was what she considered her baseline. She attended University of Missouri for undergraduate work, which was important, as neither of her parents attended college. In fact, she was the only child in her family to obtain a degree. She went to high school to coach as she completed her masters from Indiana University where she coached gymnastics and synchronized swimming, which was her "ticket out" as she became Associate Athletic Director Then Interim Athletic Director.

What did you do differently from colleagues to get to where you are?

Cheryl looked for candidates who could do the same thing. From birth, she was very strong, determined, tenacious, and relentless to challenge. She was always going to the next step and competitive along each step. That is one part of herself that she admits must remain "in check."

Who or What has been your greatest inspiration?

Age 1-10 greatest inspirations were her parents and sister

Age 11-20 – Alice Pither, a coach and teacher

"In every job, I had great mentors – Dr. Condoleezza Rice, Jenny Dutch who was at Oregon State. These were people who helped with me any aspect of the job by helping to think through problems, provide honest feedback, and always answered my call on the first ring." Admittedly a bit of a "stinker," Cheryl was always independent and at times too smart for her own good, which was picked up by her grandson who is said to be just like her. "I had great parents who told me I could do anything I wanted to do." That made her a sponge, ready to absorb and give, engage differently, and be highly energetic when doing it.

Caroline Adams Miller, another researcher, author with one of the first Masters in Positive Psychology, states, "The topic of grit evokes such strong feelings from people." What does that mean to you?

Determination, tenacity relentlessness, inner drive. Cheryl mentioned being achievement-oriented by the age of 10. It is important to have a plan of action, energy, and drive. That is why the following is critical: I always got 7 hours of sleep, ensuring the energy to go at the necessary pace; Workout daily from 5-5:30am; Very efficient with time management, understanding of organizational process; Understand/leverage people, processes, and structure.

Stories of female grit...your grittiest moments to date?

Always as a female in this role, always proving yourself, proving your worth – constant requirement of grit – like a race of endurance. There is half pound of grit needed just to maintain acceptance. Firing football coaches who are very "traditional" in their thinking/behavior, dealing with presidents asking you to do something that violates your core values and having to decide to leave. "I have to be able to look my two girls in the face."

What has been your greatest winning accomplishment so far?

She immediately mentions both career and personal. First, her position at Stanford, working her way up to second in command where she became the COO of Athletics, managing a large budget, a variety of sports, and creating a culture that led to numerous championships. She credits working in a good organization, with a great structure, remarkable processes, and people led to an unstoppable culture. She then credits her then boss, Condoleezza Rice, for her leadership and mentorship. Such excellence did not come by happenstance. She received great mentorship from Jerry Porras, co-author of Built to Last, one of the bestselling business books of all times. An unparalleled opportunity, weekly coaching sessions surrounding implementing the proven, successful habits of "enduringly" exceptional companies studied in their six-year research study. Twelve years at Stanford, hit two strategic plans, won more NCAA championships than any in history. The success model was built from scratch and used later to implement a successful football program from 2009-2018, Double A to moving to a larger conference. This was a huge checkoff for the bucket list. The other greatest accomplishment is raising two very successful daughters. Because of Cheryl's work, her daughters were raised on university campuses, taught by Olympic coaches, and got to experience culture. They saw their mother "work her butt off yet hit a glass ceiling." Cheryl is now a nationally renowned executive coach, working with Chief Financial Officers (CFOs) and Chief Operations Officers (COOs) across the nation. One day, she was in the midst of a coaching session that was pretty intense, and her daughter overheard just enough of the conversation to have an "aha" moment, telling her mother, "I had no idea all of my life we were being trained by you." Definitely a memorable moment for Cheryl.

Mentorship vs. Sponsorship –what is the difference?

Mentors see what others can be and where they can go and what they can do. It is important to double what "our" generation did. Things are improving, as demonstrated by the fact that the last three placements in AD roles were female, and it was my pleasure to mentor them and be with them every step of the way. Critical is confidence and competence. Yes, many have the degrees and the necessary experience, however you only have 3-5 seconds to demonstrate an air of confidence. When working with clients, Cheryl starts with a self-analysis grid which assess triggers, management style, it is then easier, after just a couple of sessions, to determine the strengths and weaknesses that must be addressed, meaning that you break down what they are doing wrong and train them out of it – they cannot be wimps. Cheryl began executive coaching in higher education; however, she has assisted those in private/corporate industries. This is also the reason she teaches executive classes, where I follow similar practices for improvement.

Can you describe the uniqueness of your role or a career relative to women?

There is a glass ceiling in collegiate athletics, particularly as a female AD, Division I with football responsibilities. There is only 1 of 5 across the nation with those duties, which "frustrates me because there needs to be more." This changed a bit, not a lot, after Stanford. Cheryl went on to be the AD for St. Louis University and Santa Clara without football, then went to University of Maryland, and worked for Deborah Yall where she was given some operational football duties. She would receive numerous calls for AD positions, but told people, "When you really have a job, call me." She later received a call to oversee Georgia State University to start a football team. She went, and was very successful, as the team made it to a Bowl game for two years.

If we are to make strides towards Fortune's goal of 100X25, we must:

Developing more women through training and specific placement of opportunities. Currently the ratio of male to females is 2:1.

Is this possible in your industry…why?

Yes. We must partner and include great men, with whom I am working and who are personally determined to identify high potential female performers and necessary additional training.

Favorite book of all times and why?

Built to Last – it has its own shelf, is signed by Jerry, and still contains old Post-it-notes.

When I am not working, I am:

Working out, with family – with grandsons. Two Fridays per month at noon, only work 6-8 hours with one or both. A self-proclaimed workaholic. "I am up at the crack of dawn which helps to maximize my time…very efficient."

When equating my life and success to a real person or fictitious character, I would choose:

Right from wrong.

Lisa Stephens Anderson, President

Q Point Health

Best childhood memories.

Lisa's parents were very young, 20 years of age, when they had her. She "grew up" with them. Her parents were in college and they were still learning life. They played tennis, and engaged in downhill skiing, which taught me that "if you want to do something, you can do it. You control your own destiny and if you want something, want life to take a different path, you have to create it." There was no pushing or pressure like today.

What were your favorite games to play growing up? Do any of those relate to who you are or what you do today?

Outside games were preferred, although it was very cold in North Dakota. In the winter, there was sledding, ice skating, skiing, while maximizing the summer – playing softball, outside until 10pm. Lisa shared that she and her girlfriend organized a lemonade stand and placed it across the street from the golf course in second grade. Lisa spent time talking with people while selling the lemonade, people would buy out of kindness. Some would ask, "Does your dad have a beer instead of the lemonade?" but he never sold it. They were wildly successfully at what would be her future in the business world, and she is still friends with her childhood business partner. Her grandparents had a farm which she would stay on for two weeks out of the year, spending a lot of time outside, in the barn and garden, with cats and kittens, and in the hayloft with books. She loved books. "It was my time by myself which I still need when it is time to recharge." Her favorites were Nancy Drew and Little House on the Prairie.

From the movie "Fallen," can you define what moment this was for you?

Lisa got married young, at age 22, had a son at 25, and was divorced at 27. "I realized everything from that. From that point forward, I realized I had tremendous responsibility and no plan B at the time. I had a young child and no luxury of feeling sorry for myself."

What jobs or experiences contributed the most to your success? Why?

When a junior in high school, her mother took a job in Mesa, AZ following her divorce to father. She was given an option at 16 to stay in North Dakota but visit her mother in Arizona. Lisa experienced the palm trees and ASU campus. She decided to pursue a degree in Political Science at Arizona State University and was planning to attend law school. "I knew early on that I wanted to be a lawyer" but met my first husband. There were even plans to move to Washington, D.C., but instead she took a job with a Senator in Phoenix. "I got the paying job, found my way into healthcare while he started his own business." After 10 years, Lisa went back to school and studied

Educational Leadership at Northern Arizona University where she worked throughout her schooling in administrative support positions in the healthcare industry, as there were no jobs in the field of political science. She spent 25 years at two companies, the third company was Samaritan, which became Banner Tri-West. She went back to Banner, starting in an individual contributor role with increased responsibility from manager to director to vice president to chief operations officer, and then chief executive officer of a division at Banner. Recently, she received a position as President of the Equality Health division.

The climb to success – If someone else were to tell your accomplishments, what would they say? What would the list entail?

Pivotal to her success was the position at Tri West, where she served a total of 10.5 years, however made a name for herself within four months by winning a large Department of Defense contract, which doubled the size of the organization. She led the required expansion and contract implementation - bringing up the contract in 21 states with more than 60 contractors within nine months. This was the biggest increase in her scope of responsibilities to date and propelled her career to next level.

What did you do differently from colleagues to get to where you are?

She has often contemplated this question…as "there are so many smart people and so much to know and there is always someone smarter than me, however, I can be bold, unafraid to do something that hasn't been done. "She loves to use the white board for planning, drawing pictures because it simplifies things and you do not see obstacles as a stopping point. It prompts you to ask, why can't we do this? Is it people, resources, processes, or technology?

Who or What has been your greatest inspiration?

Her son, who is now 24. The amazing people with whom she has worked. She was housed at the division headquarters where there was a female CEO in 1992 who would wear 3-piece suits, broaches, and scarves and was very smart. She has remarried a wonderful man with children and watching how kids solve problems; it helps her to remember that "there is always a solution."

What characteristics do you possess the most?

Confidence is what Lisa has worked the hardest at. "We think we have to be perfect, but we do not." There is always going to be someone better at something. She became very adept of not letting anything get in her way, and at the lowest points, it is important to remember that "everything can be solved with sleep…the sun does come back up. This gives a totally different perspective and you again realize that you can control your own destiny.

Stories of female grit...your grittiest moments to date?

During her stint at Tri West when the new DOD contract had just been won, she reviewed the requirements with the executive sponsor. She said to him, "Well, this isn't possible, we need to go back to the DOD." He allowed her to go on for approximately five minutes. A retired Army Colonel who then said to her that her "whining time was over, now you need to focus on how to get this done." It was an uphill climb, but she was able to get the team to the top by successfully leading the implementation across 21 states successfully.

How did you find your sponsor, coach, or mentor?

Lisa refers to a few people from whom she learned. First, Bill, who was instrumental early in her career and helped her move from focusing on tasks to focusing on people. He taught her how to appreciate the power of people and how people must be prioritized first. Title and background do not matter, you can learn from every single person, promoting the power of team. Second, the gentleman she reported to at Samaritan then moved to Tri West. He pushed her to attend school and provided opportunities that were developmental and career changing. Although at certain times, it was important to be rough and tough, especially on the insurance side. She learned that sometimes you must decide, but when you do, default to what is best for your people and your clients. Third was Vilma. Later in her career it was necessary to get a nanny. Lisa felt fortunate to be able to afford such support and fortunate to get Vilma. Vilma traveled with her and she came to admire Vilma, from El Salvador, as she learned a different language and culture. Vilma was instrumental in helping to raise her son and although the son is grown, Vilma is still part of the family. She brings joy to everyone in her life. Last but not least is her mom who happens to be the grittiest person she knows. Her mother was the seventh eldest child. She put herself through college and studied Accounting & Finance. She was the first female partner & CFO of a hospital system.

What are some words of wisdom and no-nonsense advice you have received?

A former CEO of Banner was very tough and faced with one of the greatest financial challenges in history. How do you address the issues while keeping the team motivated? Lisa would soon find out. She had to stand in front of the entire organization and provide an update regarding the financial crisis. Her boss was in the room and at the conclusion of Lisa's speech, she said" You just won their hearts and minds." This was the moment she realized that it is not important to be the strongest person in the room every day, but it is important to show vulnerability at times.

That experience and feedback from the team paid off. The team operated at a different level and maximized the opportunity, therefore maximizing the power of the team.

If we are to make strides towards Fortune's goal of 100X25, we must:

Reverse the funnel, as you are going up, much smaller pool, deliberate decisions and sponsorships by CEOs. Set a goal. Be public about the commitment. It must be supported by leadership and boards – the deficit of women on public and private boards is well known. Establish deliberate targets with detailed strategies and publish as part of quarterly earnings report.

Is this possible in your industry...why?

There are numerous women in healthcare, but the C-Suite still has a significant gap in the workforce. Traditional roles of finance, more leadership positions are occurring in other industries, but not in healthcare.

Essential daily or weekly reads:

Focus on national headlines; Listens to NPR in the car daily; Receives newspaper per week; Online CNN daily; local news

What do women need to do more of to reach the highest levels in corporate America or beyond?

Support one another; understand the path for the position that you are seeking; make sure the glass ceiling at least has a hole large enough for others to break through.

What do women need to do less of to reach the highest levels or corporate America?

Stop doubting themselves; stop holding back!

Favorite movie of all times and why?

Romantic comedies – "Love Actually", "You've Got Mail", "27 dresses"

Favorite book of all times and why?

Lisa loves books – mysteries, fiction, leadership. Dare to Lead and any Malcolm Gladwell book. Lisa and her husband are part of a book club and read together every evening before going to bed.

Favorite quote?

"Many may forget what you said, but not how you made them feel."

When I am not working, I am:

Spending time with the people I love.

It is essential for women to know....and do:

Sleep – all of life's problems can be solved with sleep; it provides a fresh perspective.

If I could redo/relive a professional moment, it would be:

A time when I did not remember or live up to Maya Angelou's quote as I was task-oriented and did not value people over tasks. Life is a learning process, both professionally and personally. Both she and her husband are doing quite a bit, and things are not perfect; every now and then there is a store-bought pie that perhaps did not look as home baked as she would have liked. While her husband compliments her by saying, "I don't know how she does it all – books, working mom, high level job" but what she realizes that you are doing it all, there is balance, and although her son's baby book is not done and he is 21 years old, he's okay.

People would be surprised if they knew I:

"Just celebrated my eleventh wedding anniversary." She and her husband attended junior high and high school together and reconnected at their 20-year high school reunion.

Best piece of business advice I ever received came from?

Bill Vandenbosh – "You know you can't control everything."

Terry Roman, Partner
Snell & Wilmer

Best childhood memories.

"We sometimes undervalue where we have been," said Terry. She described being part of a typical middle-class family – both good and bad, but stable. The third of four children, she knew at an early age she wanted to be a lawyer, which was unusual as she grew up in the mid-west – St. Louis, Missouri, and Webster Groves, Missouri, where women were "boxed in." It was interesting that the thought popped into her head between fifth. and eighth grade, which garnered a very "weird reaction" from those around her.

Favorite games to play growing up? Do any of those relate to who you are or what you do today?

Games – running games, chase with a gang of kids. Terry describes growing up during a time when Title IX was adopted, providing equity to girls relative to sports. So, Terry became involved in tennis and gymnastics.

From the movie "Fallen," can you define what moment this was for you?

When coming to Arizona for college at the University of Arizona not knowing anyone. Realizing at this point that her upbringing in the mid-west was a bit sheltered. On the airplane with suitcases and tears. She remembers sobbing to a girl, a complete stranger, as she realized she was on her own and way out in Arizona with no one. It made her stronger.

Your educational and work experience – what jobs or experiences contributed the most to your success? Why?

Terry came up during a time of significant change for women – the passage of Title IX in 1975, increased number of women attending college (tons at U of A), and a number of women graduating from undergraduate and going on to graduate school. Terry estimated that approximately 40% of those in law school her first year were women. She realized that she went the unsafe route but was determined to fulfill her dream. She worked really, really, really hard, built a network, and joined Snell & Wilmer, the #2 law firm in Arizona and has worked there for 35 years.

If your career could be told in a story, what would be the conflict, climax, the antagonist and what do you project to be a happy ending?

In 1982, 15 people joined Snell and half were women. Three are still there and two are partners. Other career highlights included Senate Judiciary committee hearings, then the most critical one, Justice Sandra Day O'Conner's confirmation hearing through Senator DeConcini, with whom she was working. Prior to Terry joining Snell, there may have been one female partner, which makes her accomplishment of partner at the age of 30 even more extraordinary. Her explanation…" I worked really, really, hard." At that time, she had no kids and was single. She began to specialize in mergers and acquisition, a very complex and high-pressure type of law. There had not been instances where men did not want her on the deal, however there was a top attorney on a case and an older incident when she was transitioning as the lead/top attorney, and an older gentleman client had to adjust and get past the fact that she was a "cute young thing." This expanded to her appointment to the Executive Committee. There are always questions surrounding women's toughness and perception of bossy or bitchy.

The climb to success – If someone else were to tell your accomplishments, what would they say? What would the list entail?

Best transaction healthcare attorney in the city. To motivate herself and remember what she is capable of, she rubs her hands together and says, "Come on Terry."

What did you do differently from colleagues to get to where you are?

She worked really hard, created a definite theme for her life. She learned to trust her own judgement and advice as her mom was not a "hovering mother." This has helped her success. Deal with bullies, using both a light and heavy hand. This could also require throwing down the "F" bomb.

Who or what has been your greatest inspiration?

Terry is self-motivated and inspired. She grew up psyching herself up, therefore she often inspired herself. In addition, her father was hard working, got up, traveled, and ingrained hard work with the family.

What does Grit mean to you?

"Scrappy resonates with me." That is who she is on a daily basis, putting one foot in front of the other.

Which characteristics do you most represent?

Most – optimism and confidence – Terry will buy an old car and fix it/rework it.

Least – Perfection – not pragmatic; great judgement, logical, linear in thought so she is not aspiring for this at all.

"I want every one of you to become the subject of someone else's story of overcoming." What does this mean to you?

In the office, the women at Snell constantly have one another's back, constantly supporting. Always looking for opportunities to help the other women shine. For example, a major event where the woman planning had a last-minute emergency. "We stepped in." Terry shared instances where they have assisted with one another's children. There is great confidence in the human spirit.

If you had to do something all over again, good or bad, what would it be?

So glad I went to law school. No regrets there. "When I consider success, some women marry men that love them in spite of what they do and who they are. I am married to a man who married me particularly because of what I do and who I am."

If we are to make strides towards Fortune's goal of 100X25, we must:

Educate some of the men and garner their support.

Chris Krueger

Senior Vice President, Banking

Best childhood memories.

Chris described her fondest memories as those from her grandma's house, eating Whoppers and juicy fruit. In the pantry was everything imaginable. She also reflected lovingly on the fact that her grandmother had hair down her back, which Chris was able to brush. Her grandmother "always had time for everyone and came to the US from Germany at the age of 17 with her brother, not speaking any English."

Favorite games to play growing up? Do any of those relate to who you are or what you do today?

Chris was a leader even at a young age. Her favorite game was playing school and she would be the one determining the day's game agenda – "What are we going to do and what are the rules?" This absolutely aligns with current role and desire. Having had a daughter at the age of 17, Chris had to immediately and suddenly grow up to support her child. She married, but he did not contribute much. Further, her parents were not supportive, always worried, and reminded her that it was not too late for an abortion. She said to them, "I thought you were Christians." Making it even more difficult was the fact that she was a straight-A student with honors, but more challenging than anything was the fact that her father would not speak to her. "Dad would not speak to me, he was very involved in church, but was definitely shunning me once he knew I was pregnant."

What jobs or experiences contributed the most to your success? Why?

Needing to do what it takes to make a life for herself, she started working the morning shift at Coco's at 5:30am, where several wealthy gentlemen had breakfast. It so happened that one owned a bank and thought her customer service skills and personality would illuminate in the banking field. When offered the opportunity, she exclaimed, "Oh, that would be awesome." She started as a teller, then new account representative, receptionist, Assistant Manager, Manager – she was there for 10 years. She then went to a different bank.

If your career could be told in a story, what would be the conflict, climax, the antagonist and what do you project to be a happy ending?

Conflict occurred as sexual harassment, totally a man's world, especially in small community banks. "Honey, are you really a good girl, let's go to Vegas, run off to Mexico." Chris reports a time in her career where she was not feeling fully competent, but was responsible for commercial clients, Operations – reviewing deposit accounts for anything suspicious – even dollar deposits and transactions. This is actually a point where she informed the EVP that something was going on. "I think he's kiting checks." Chris had to take it to the President, as she had an intuition that this was broader. It turned out she was right. All three banks lost money, including her bank, to the tune of $2M. The president was unsure, but because of the involvement of the FBI, there was not as much of a concern. This was not the only incident; another would arise later, and the response would be, "We are shutting this down." Jim went to prison and actually died in prison. The president shared the issue with the board, but it was easier to blame others rather than one of the "good ole' boys."

What did you do differently from colleagues to get to where you are?

Relationships that were built and ways in which she was able to see and utilize others' value. This is the true measure of leadership, gendering someone who has talent, making them standout. There are a lot of egos in banking. Chris then remembers a young lady on the team who was very intelligent, knowledgeable, but rough around the edges. This was an incredible opportunity to develop another woman for leadership opportunities.

Who or What has been your greatest inspiration?

The greatest inspiration has been from the relationships built. People who when contacted, would, stop what they were doing, provide feedback. They were invested, confident in "me," yet hands off. One of the early managers in her career, Mary, who carried herself in a consummate professional manner and whom she still sees today, supported her more than anyone with emphasis on the following:

- Always do the right thing
- Own up to things when you should
- Recognize the problem and how/who should be involved in solving

What does Grit mean to you?

Tenacity, sticking to whatever it is you are going after and having a little bit of sass.

Which characteristics do you possess most?

Optimism – positive attitude, believing that you can – creativity is just operating in non-conventional ways when getting things accomplished although you may be in non-conventional industry.

Excellence & Perfection: "I thought I was a failure as it was taking a long time to get over things. I realized excellence does not mean you get everything right or the process smooth, but the result is pretty darn amazing. You can get to excellence." "Common sense is a superpower."

Stories of female grit...your grittiest moments to date?

There were numerous times when she refused to do deposits for very powerful people or allow processes that were incompatible with corporate standards and requirements.

What has been your greatest winning accomplishment so far?

Making Senior Vice President had previously earned VP title years prior.

What are some Words of Wisdom and no-nonsense advice you have received?

Wisdom – "Always do the right thing." Nonsense – "Your whole life is over now," at age 17. What was sad was that she believed it. If she had a theme song it would be "How you like me now?" by The Heavy.

If we are to make strides towards Fortune's goal of 100X25, we must:

Not a lot of women CEOs in banking. The biggest thing is to get other women to encourage one another. "It can be back-stabby instead, but instead of competition, women have relationship building capabilities in their favor. Women should definitely play to their strengths."

Essential daily or weekly reads:

Crossword puzzles daily to keep the mind active and enhance vocabulary. I read all of the time and love to read. All books (500) are on the iPad. "I even read when I work out!

Favorite movie of all times and why?

"Steele Magnolias", which made her laugh and cry. It provides an ideal of how women should be – strong, having each other's back.

Favorite book of all times and why?

The Stand – Stephen King – good versus evil with several stories tying together including the little old lady in Nebraska, which is where Chris was born.

Favorite quote?

Theodore Roosevelt – The Man in the Arena

"It is not the critic who counts; not the man who points out how the strong man stumbles, or where the doer of deeds could have done them better. The credit belongs to the man who is actually in the arena, whose face is marred by dust and sweat and blood; who strives valiantly; who errs, who comes short again and again, because there is no effort without error and shortcoming; but who does actually strive to do the deeds; who knows great enthusiasms, the great devotions; who spends himself in a worthy cause; who at the best knows in the end the triumph of high achievement, and who at the worst, if he fails, at least fails while daring greatly, so that his place shall never be with those cold and timid souls who neither know victory nor defeat."

When I am not working, I am:

Reading

When equating my life and success to a real person or fictitious character, I would choose:

Eleanor Roosevelt

People would be surprised if they knew I:

Have seven grandchildren

Michelle Halyard

Dean of the Arizona Campus, Mayo Medical School

Best childhood memories.

Michelle grew up as an only child, and therefore, her greatest memories are with her cousins. She was in Buffalo and her cousins were in Pittsburgh where they spent time.

What were your favorite games to play growing up? Do any of those relate to who you are or what you do today?

Michelle remembers amazing family picnics in Kennywood; playing hide and seek; roaming her neighborhood. Her mother was protective so when she was with her cousins she could venture out.

From the movie "Fallen," can you define what moment this was for you?

It occurred when she was divorcing the kid's dad and trying to keep the family intact although the time was being split. At the same time, her mother was diagnosed with Alzheimer's. This triggered a deepening of faith. "I would never have met Kevin or selflessness."

What jobs or experiences contributed the most to your success? Why?

At nine years of age, Michelle was diagnosed with Vitiligo where she had spots on her hand and face during her middle school years. Depigmentation when 12 years old shapes you and actually gave her sensitivity to others. Impact? "As a young black lady, I had to find ways to identify in other ways, however, things change as I got older. Attending a Historically Black College or University was helpful as there was no one judging whether or not I was good enough, and more importantly, there is no self-doubt, helping to build a sense of self confidence and getting a tremendous start." Michelle thought she wanted to go to Georgetown, however the admissions and interview process was less than welcoming. She was told, "Maybe you need to declare a different major." It just so happened one of her neighbors attended Georgetown and would provide insight. However, through that process Michelle discovered the six-year accelerated program at Howard University where she excelled. Michelle needed a fellowship, more oncology training, figured out last year what was needed, and Mayo happened to have a slot in Rochester, MN. She called and they accepted her for what was scheduled to be one year. However, she absolutely loved it and stayed for two. She was twelfth of 2000 residents. Again, she went on to excel, deciding to interview at Mayo in Arizona.

If your career could be told in a story, what would be the conflict, climax, the antagonist and what do you project to be a happy ending?

Starting at Mayo in radiation oncology focused on breast, head, and neck. One year later, Michelle joined the Diversity committee and later became the chair, later conducted the institutional cultural audit, and was placed in front of the Board of Governors (Mayo Board of Directors) in the fourth year then asked to join the Board of Governors her fifth year.

The climb to success – If someone else were to tell your accomplishments, what would they say? What would the list entail?

The rigor of the Howard residency was critical to Michelle's success, especially as she transitioned to Mayo. Her journey was one where her competence would be tapped right away as a former nun in charge of diversity in Minnesota asked her to join the diversity committee, giving her access to the Executive committee and Board of Trustees. She then began chairing a department, interacting with the Board of Trustees and the Board of Governors early in her career which allowed her to build institutional credibility. Mayo then had a tri-site cancer center in Arizona, Minnesota, and Florida where Michelle would act as Leadership Development Physician. Following that stint, she came off the local board 2002/2003 to focus on research and gaining full professorship. In 2013, she joined the medical school because she liked creating new things and was encouraged to apply for the deanship. Fred Meyer was the dean of three campuses, and Mayo is the only multistate medical school. Others such as Morehouse, Meharry, Drew, UC Irvine all have women deans. "When a door opens, I walk through it." In terms of plans, retirement or a higher level. If considering a role such as

CEO of Arizona Mayo, I had to determine what personal costs I wanted to pay. Because I did not want to move to Rochester, the roles became limited.

What did you do differently from colleagues to get to where you are?

Never felt or dwelt on gender or race differences. Guys have more of a network, but I have developed my own.

Who or What has been your greatest inspiration?

Michelle is inspired by the love of her patients, getting up making a difference every day. Also, an inspiration are young people who are energetic. She spends a great deal of time with mentees, very diverse and quite a number of students of color. An institution, university, or organization is greater with greater diversity. This helps open the institution to people who are not normally there.

What characteristics do you possess?

Courage – "I don't feel like I have anything to lose. Very little fear telling people what I think." The message must be tempered differently based on how the audience will receive it. Resilience and the ability to know that everything will be fine and see the connectedness with it all, bringing together all these traits.

Stories of female grit...your grittiest moments to date?

Conflict with the Board of Governors/Trustees, Arizona President, CEO Rochester, creating variable fractions – all men, "It was a mess." Michelle acted as a mediator and said, "You can destroy the organization or cut it out." Well aware that she was the most senior woman and a black woman, 25 years senior, but they had "tapped my last nerve," she said.

What has been your greatest winning accomplishment so far?

Reputation and her ability to build a team and go to bat for what is right. Respected within the organization. "I did not focus on if people liked me, I gave up on that a long time ago," she says and attributes it to her personality developed from being an only child.

Did/do you have a sponsor, coach or mentor? If so, what do you believe is the most valuable information you have gleaned or help you were given?

Dr. Viva Pinn, Chair – Department of Pathology Howard, National Institute of Health

What are some words of wisdom and no-nonsense advice you have received?

Michelle's mom imparted the importance of integrity. In addition, Dr. LaSalle Leffall, Chair of Surgery, said "Equanimity under duress." He would know because he ended up being the first African American President of the American Cancer Society.

If you had to do something all over again, good or bad, what would it be?

Michelle married the first time at 24, thinking at the time that "I needed a relationship to be complete." She soon realized her own value without being attached.

Can you describe the uniqueness of your role or a career relative to women?

The convergence of academics and medicine. American Association of Medical Colleges talk about issues that arise for the purpose of mid-career development, forums discussing the local work environment, a very grassroots approach – making yourself. Not all women feel obligated to get in the game to help promote other women. Michelle is passionate about trying to help other women and she does not diminish her passion and has been told "you need to be more kitteny." As you can imagine, this did not go over well with Michelle. There are 150 medical schools with less than 5% enrollment for women.

If we are to make strides towards Fortune's goal of 100X25, we must:

Michelle described a "Lean In" event she attended in Rochester where one of the speakers was Ursula Burns, former CEO Xerox. Through this conversation her stories were relived and therefore, validated through the lives of others. Issues such as not knowing if an idea was meritorious or not. The first thing that pops into your head is "not." This appears to be a gender issue, not race issue. Enterprise white males went for the same position as Michell, Executive Dean of the Medical school. Michelle has non-negotiables and is known for disruptive change, which often results in not being selected, however response was, "It just wasn't meant to be."

What do women need to do more of to reach the highest levels in corporate America or beyond?

Stretch beyond their comfort zones and not take yourself out of the game. Women often focus on what they do not have. "I don't have this, no experience in that" while men will throw their hat into the ring. So, take risks and get your name out there.

It is essential for women to know….and do:

Work life balance; figure out how to integrate as much as you can. "I think of it as a teeter totter." Initially she felt tremendous guilt having to hire a nanny, who turned out to be excellent and even a second parent to the children. You bury a lot of emotion and try not to think of it. Remote access is not always good pathology of life. "I wanted to come home and have dinner" and then went back to work.

When I was at a low point, even my lowest point, it was important that I do:

Go to church and pray

When equating my life and success to a real person or fictitious character, I would choose:

Condoleezza Rice – only child, smart, achieved at a young age and certain heights at five – piano and music theory

People would be surprised if they knew I:

Michelle graduated at the age of 19 with strengths in writing, English and verbal. Her Mom taught at Buffalo University and Michelle was going to follow in the footsteps and become a teacher. Her mother was diagnosed with cancer in her early forties and had five mastectomy surgeries, very mutilating. That led her to wanting to conduct quality of life research. Her mom later asked surprisingly, "You want to be a doctor"? Her father died in 1988; quite a bit of loss for anyone, especially an only child.

Best piece of business advice I ever received came from?

The Chair of the department she joined when entering Mayo. Narcissistic is how she would describe him which made it a rough transition. The Chief Administrative Officer who had a PhD in Finance told her, "Stiffen your back, it's going to get worse before it gets better, pull up your big girl panties and buck up."

Kim Dartez

Compass Dartez, Founder & CEO

Best childhood memories.

Kim's mom did crafts, paper balloons, and nativity scene. Her mom had a big creative influence in her life growing up.

Favorite games to play growing up? Do any of those relate to who you are or what you do today?

Monopoly. Her mom's friend Denice had an elaborate Monopoly game.

From the movie "Fallen," can you define what moment this was for you?

I believe I am being used by God to give his children their inheritance, prophetic events. There was also a "pie" lady who lived in Tempe where olive trees were prohibited, yet trees were full of olives for 15 years. Normally, trees are dormant for seven years…so many times, confirmation of fruitfulness. In 2009, released balloon at the homegoing and gave her life to the Lord, New Year's morning.

Your educational and work experience – what jobs or experiences contributed the most to your success? Why?

As an assistant, Kim was not intimidated by others with higher level positions. She got involved with women of color, realizing she was not alone in experiences and that there needed to be a national movement. Kim worked in both the for-profit and non-profit arenas. There is a medical clinic on Central & Baseline where suddenly in that area ovarian cancer spiked, illustrating common health disparities. "We have to conquer this on all levels. As an African American population, we eat, sleep, pay bills, die early, young survivors of domestic violence and working living wage jobs." Her family tree is filled with healthcare advocates/professionals. Her mom was responsible for bringing black nurses to Arizona. Following her mom's death, she transitioned to domestic violence advocacy in the community of color, focusing on resources and availability of services. In 2009, funding was taken away from special communities as there was no representation. She thought it was important to support facilitation groups Kim for victims. Simultaneously, was assistant to the first female engineer. It is here where she became interested in construction and identified a way to support employment within the African American community. There were major construction projects being undertaken that required the state to diversify its vendor base.

Stories of female grit…your grittiest moments to date?

Fran was an older woman, early 30s at the time, an activist who asked Michelle, "Why are you so mad, everybody's suffering." Kim says that she became a raging Fran to fight disparities in health, administration of services, employment injustices. Everyone can see but people are operating in silos. 20 years ago, there was planning for Loop 202. The project was bid out to three joint ventures for $1.6 Billion. The State awarded the Loop 202 to a firm headquartered out of Tennessee. The primary launched outreach across states for subcontractors to no avail. "All plans out the window," a DBE (Disadvantaged Business Enterprise) goal of $20 million. Still no significant progress made and the challenges leading to the lack of progress were supported by State officials. Kim contacted the federal government and called for an investigation.

What has been your greatest winning accomplishment so far?

Me! Evolving as an activist and raising my amazing sons.

What is the greatest difference between you and your male counterpart, if any?

Her husband is white, and she is black. His father was the Grand Dragon of the KKK. Her husband still worries about this.

Essential daily or weekly reads:

Daily devotional. Social justice issues; ACES childhood trauma matrix.

What do women need to do less of to reach the highest levels or corporate America?

Support each other rather than compete

Favorite movie of all times and why?

"The Matrix – Unplug." When a system is unhealthy, unplug.

Favorite book of all times and why?

Joy Dugrew, Post Traumatic Slave Disorder

When equating my life and success to a real person or fictitious character, I would choose:

Harriett Tubman

People would be surprised if they knew I:

Kim says she is a cry baby, very emotional. She started a non-profit in support of the Violence Against Women's Act. Creating a state coalition with national connection because of discrimination being reported in the shelters. There was also discrimination in how law enforcement handled incidents as they were told to arrest them both.

Launching shelter report groups was essential to programming and to the healing of the victims' release of anger, however, did not allow cursing. In working with the National Center Call to Acton Women of Color Network which was federally funded. Heightened attention was given to Arizona in 2008 during the Super Bowl and a special taskforce was formulated to campaign against domestic and sexual violence during the event. Tony Porter, football players and wives participated. The work was so impressive that others took credit for it during a luncheon with Roger Goddell's wife to which she was not even invited. Kim would not be deterred. She started another initiative on "how to identify domestic violence parenting program" which received $300K funding. Kim's other business: Construction. She is the only black woman who owns a construction business. Because she noticed men were perpetrating violence, going to jail then being unable to find work, she would get them into construction. Further, she worked with the Arizona Commerce Authority for those released from prison to help build apartments but could not settle on a reasonable amount. She cited research that mentioned the correlation between the number of prison beds and 8th grade suspension and ethnicity to economic stream. Fees and fines are also discriminatory in nature as the State claims harm and the violators to get paid for restitution. Kim went on to get business certificate and positioned herself to work on major projects. She has built relationships – McCarthy, Philips, Hewitt, and Hunt, along with the first female commissioner for the State of Arizona, Colonel Wanda Wright. Kim's theme now – "How you like me now?" She admits, "I'm not a republican nor am I all the way to the left." She sees her role as reaching out to municipalities to improve the lives of economically disadvantaged.

Best piece of business advice I ever received came from?

Corey Foster – Arizona Department of Transportation – "Always trust your gut" "Integrity is #1, whatever level in life."

Kathy

Chief Technology Officer

Kathy sat down with us, and instead of an interview, she shared over coffee her keys to living a life with grit as a woman. She offers her introspective perspective on how to be successful woman in the C Suite.

Kathy says the key is "getting over the emotional," which immediately causes males to lose respect and "having too much," passion which can cause one to lose her focus. She continues, "Focus is critical, self-focus, so that you are able to see your way through the frustrating times to serve others in spite of [it]. That respect for others will ultimately result in meaningful meetings where you are given true insight into the business, your team members will pick up at 2am, all of which will force or propel the woman to the top of the company." Kathy believes women operate from a perspective of empathy and altruism, and her goal is "to leave this life and be known for service I gave this world."

Meg Whitman, who was of the CEOs of a Fortune 500, truly a private club, decided to step down, as did Pepsi Co's CEO, Indra Nooyi. Why? They had been successful, very balanced yet were asked to do something they were not in agreement with. Top women do not get into such a quandary without realizing the balance between confidence, egotism, and arrogance that can lead to a completely different conversation. They have another side. They are not willing to put up with unethical requests.

As a woman, it is even more important to have structured thinking. As a matter of fact, she has become more structured in her thinking in her later years and has become good in all IT disciplines, even coding. However, she prefers larger concepts and strategy, and correlates learning engineering to learning life. Staying innovative, being inventive and serving as an excellent strategist. It is not uncommon to find younger women CEOs, and when we do, they are engineers by training. "We did not have any of that when I was younger," says Kathy.

Kathy did not pursue college and has learned everything hands-on by teaching herself. When attempting college in her younger years, she was undisciplined and would cram for exams. Now, "I read every day – spiritual books of the world, advance quantum fields, big bang and different dimensions." She recalls taking an online course, History of Advanced Mathematics, with an Australian professor with other physics content where God and science fit. That fit with her long-time desire to bend the two together.

Growing up around boys, she saw her mom stay at home and wanted to be more like her father, who was an electrical superintendent. Kathy believes grit comes from a desire to survive. Having grown up in a neighborhood full of boys, she did not see herself different. Contrarily, she used it to her advantage and learned to play golf and pursued a job at the Marriott, as that provided free balls and golf. Noted as great worker, they continued to support her. She left home before graduating from high school. Kathy decided to pursue professional golf, where she became one of the first female golf pros but was also recognized as being business savvy. This was proven out as she took a very difficult exam and passed the first time when others took on average two to three times. The first-time failure rate was 70%. No one had spoken with her about the test. Kathy operates from the belief that you can do whatever you want. Whatever we do as women, it has to be with grit and for the purpose of service.

"If they are not going to promote you, go somewhere else," she was told. She shares how she went into the president to inform him that she was doing the same job as her peers and should be recognized and compensated as such. They agreed. This taught her how important it is to be assertive.

Kathy has always been involved in industries primarily dominated by men, as a CTO, CIO, and golf pro. She has spent a great deal of her career on organizational "turn arounds" and mentoring others.

Kathy was influenced by a gentleman she worked for, a very successful physicist who gave up his entire life for service. He taught her the importance of being in touch with people as a leadership strength and differentiator, also how women view themselves comes to fruition and women typically limit themselves by not realizing their capabilities. "It's your attitude that has to change. All you can do is modify how you react to the challenges. If you see yourself as Einstein, that is who you will become."

Kathy Young
Corporate Executive

Best childhood memories.

One of my sweetest memories was of my mom hand sewing Barbie outfits for Christmas one year. She did not know how to sew, and Barbie dresses were hardly available and expensive. Other ladies at her office were making Barbie cloths and they taught her how to hand stitch the cloths. Other best memories were hearing my grandma laugh. She had such a wonderful laugh, one that warmed you all over. She taught me to bake, sew and took me to her church. She made wonderful bread and so many dishes that I miss. I would take my 2 kids and drive from Phoenix to La Habra, Ca to see her. When we left, she would have a picnic 'fit for a king' for my kids and me. Her baking was a handful of this and a pinch of that. And she had so many wise words that fell on death ears at the time, but I do remember them now. She would take me to church, and everyone would stay for dinner. There were always 4 courses. The food – chia, bread, cucumbers, tomatoes, lettuce were right from their farms. Then the soup, and then the roasted meat and bread. And then finally fruit, dates and chia. Everyone would sing and talk. At the end, everyone would help wash dishes, clean up and put away all the tables. I can still smell the clean and ironed tablecloths and wonderful smells from the kitchen.

What were your favorite games to play growing up? Do any of those relate to who you are or what you do today?

My mom loved to play cards and we would play cards together when she got off from work or on the weekends. I still love to play Solitaire.

After school, I loved playing 4 Square with the neighborhood boys or Tetherball! All were then and still are so much fun.

Today, I still like to work in solitary. And when it is an option, banter and kid around with the people in the office.

Memorable moment/event as a child:

Each Halloween my mom and I would go to her friends. The boys and I would go Trick or Treating while the adults would play cards. When we got back, the boys and I would make popcorn and then sort our candy.

Philosophical/spiritual underpinnings:

Wow, this changes as you go through life, I think. I have always believed in being kind and giving to others. I cherish each the time I get to be with smart people, to listen to their stories and gather wisdom. I believe everyone is better than they think they are, and I do my best to encourage them, so they know it too.

Educational and work experiences. What jobs or experiences contributed the most to your success? Why?

I was often too deep in the details to take advantage of many of the educational offerings which was stupid on my part.

I was lucky become friends with a woman who helped me get a job at Motorola as a junior programmer. From that got the chance to go to Europe and Mexico for work. I moved on to Intel at very exciting time in the semi-conductor world. Shortly after I joined, I raised my hand to take an assignment in the U.K. with my children. What an amazing experience that was for the 3 of us. A few years later I was off to Japan and Hong Kong on another assignment. I learned so much about the differences in laws, people and traditions. I left Intel for a position at American Express where I was assigned a team who created monitoring software for terminals and networks. Eventually after many re-organizations, I became 1 of the 2 Technology Program Managers. We managed large initiatives that required coordination across hardware/software, building Call Centers, and coordinating with Technology teams. This position grew and I was promoted and given the task to create a new team of project managers who would take on additional initiatives.

If someone else were to tell your accomplishments, what would they say? What would the list entail?

I started as a computer operator. Then went on to get a position as a Jr. Programmer at Motorola. At Motorola I was asked to go to Europe to train on new software that she had created. Some friends left Motorola for Intel and found a position for her there. At Intel she worked as a programmer then SR programmer. They were looking for additional staff and she called a couple friends and they were also hired. She was offered a position in the UK for a period of time to work on a new Global Order Entry system. She and her 2 children moved Swindon UK and experienced a life abroad. A few years later she took an assignment as Manager in Japan to install another new Global Order Entry application. After 7 years at Intel, she took her 3-month paid sabbatical. After she returned from sabbatical Intel decided to move their IT department to Folsom, California. A friend decided not to move and got a job at American Express and helped her get a job there also. At American Express she had the chance to learn about networks, terminal authorization processing, risk management, new accounts, Government Credit card procurement, and other initiatives. She was eventually promoted to Director where she created a team of program managers. A few years later she took her system knowledge became an Application Architect. During the 2007 recession her entire organization was laid off from American Express, but she was able to get a year extension and work in Brighton, UK. This lasted for 18 months. A year later, she was called back as a contractor to American Express to manage the build out of hardware and software for the new Human Resource application. From there she went to work for Wells Fargo and Union Bank and found them boring compared to her previous assignments. Now she is working at a local playhouse, organizing, managing staff and taking care of customers.

What did you do differently from colleagues to get to where you are?

Said 'yes' to every door that was offered and was lucky. My desire to make a good living for my kids and myself.

What does "grit" mean to you?

No matter what the problem is make a plan and go for it. And if you are lucky, there will be someone there to help you.

What characteristics of grit do you have?

On a personal level, I am determined to see and experience all the world has to offer, enjoy my family and friends. Additionally, I think giving back to the community is important and to other less fortunate than me.

On a professional level, I like to work for well-paying companies. I strive to think of how I can help others achieve their goals. In turn, I also become successful.

How long or how many experiences did it take to ascertain this characteristic of grit/grittiness?

I was lucky (or dumb) enough not to overthink opportunities when they came knocking and just went for it.

What are your grittiest moments to date?

Getting laid off from American Express during the 2007 recession was devastating to me.

What has been your greatest winning accomplishment so far?

Mentoring a team of bright people to be their best and giving several of them their confidence back. My team was admired and thought of highly. Many went on to get promotions and all did well with their careers.

Mentorship vs. Sponsorship –what is the difference?

A mentor is often someone who provide guidance to you. A sponsor is one who looks after your career.

Did/do you have a sponsor, coach, or mentor? If so, what do you believe is the most valuable information you have gleaned or help you were given?

I had several mentors. The one who made the most impact I had for a couple years. She helped me gain my confidence, guidance and leadership skills.

How did you find your sponsor, coach, or mentor?

We worked together.

Who has contributed or what has contributed to your success more than anything?

Being single and having to make a living. I got lucky to get into technologies and get paid well. I worked extra hours to ensure I had everything completed on time.

"I want every one of you to become the subject of someone else's story of overcoming." What does this mean to you?

To become the subject of someone else's story means that you help someone realize the gifts they have and help them to recognize and appreciate their accomplishments.

What is the greatest difference between you and your male counterpart, if any?

I had such a fear of failing and often the frustration with men getting more attention. The fear of failure never went away but with time, gaining knowledge and more confidence, and talking louder, helped my male my counterparts respect my opinions.

If you had to do something all over again, good or bad, what would it be?

This is a difficult question. I dreamed of making a difference in the world of science. But I got pregnant and married at 16. The world (school, parents, work mates) said I was 'no one' and I believed it. If I could do it over, I would have focused on getting 4-year degree and focus more on my education along with caring for and raising my 2 kids.

Can you describe the uniqueness of your role or a career relative to women?

I think technologies is very receptive of women if you maintain your education, creativity and speak up. We need to focus more on the math and the sciences.

If we are to make strides towards Fortune's goal of 100X25, we must...

Women of today and the future need to decide where they want the world to be. Dominated by men making all of the decisions or owning their place at the table. We need more lawyers, doctors, executives, elected leaders and board members to make changes that reflect us all.

Is this possible in your industry...why?

It is possible but women must make more of an effort in math and the sciences to become the next 'Bill Gates' Super Star. Women must focus on math and the sciences, speak up and get published. I have read so many empty 'papers' created by men and wondered what they got credit for this 'paper'. The reason, they took time to write it. So, publish, express and speak up.

What do women need to do more of to reach the highest levels in corporate America or beyond?

First, stop underestimating themselves. Second, stop dressing like you are going out. It is work, not a dating game. Third, keep educating yourself. You must be the smartest in the room. Forth, find a mentor and surround yourself with smart people. Believe in yourself.

What do women need to do less of to reach the highest levels or corporate America?

Not just America but everywhere. Stick together and learn to be a team! Stop trying to eliminate other female competition. Find and nurture each other.

Favorite movie of all time and why?

A recent movie call Hidden Figures. The movie showed how 3 women, 2 had mentors, make such incredible impact to NASA's first moon launch and just as importantly, open the doors to women across IT. Dorothy Vaughn opened IT up for women of all color. She and her 3 friends should be our inspirations for generations to come. All smart women, all supporting each other.

Favorite book of all time and why?

Eleanor Roosevelt by Blanche Wiesen Cook – I found her to be one of the amazing women ever. She had such sadness in her life losing both parents and being raised by an unkind aunt, and then marrying an unloving husband, yet she grew to become one of the most creative, powerful and forward-thinking women. She believed in family planning, marched for the ERA, she and her friends would bring trunks full of diaphragms from Europe to support family planning. She believed in good working conditions, so she encouraged her Franklin to look at the coal mines and shorten the work week. And she believed in humanity. She worked with Einstein and others of the time to create the International Rescue Committee (IRC) and help so many who fled from war.

Favorite quote?

The future belongs to those who believe in the beauty of their dreams! Steve Jobs

When I am not working, I am:

Working and contributing

If I could redo/relive a professional moment, it would be:

Too many to list.

People would be surprised if they knew I:

I was always terrified I would fail and be poor.

References

http://www.costcoconnection.com/connection/201809?pg=51#pg51

Stevenson, J., Orr, E. (2017). We Interviewed 57 Female CEO's to Find Out How More Women Can Get to the Top. Retrieved from https://hbr.org/2017/11/we-interviewed-57-female-ceos-to-find-out-how-more-women-can-get-to-the-top

Duckworth, A. (2016). Q & A. Retrieved from https://angeladuckworth.com/qa/

Perlis, M. (2013). 5 Characteristics of Grit—How Many do You Have? Retrieved from https://www.forbes.com/sites/margaretperlis/2013/10/29/5-characteristics-of-grit-what-it-is-why-you-need-it-and-do-you-have-it/#3620244a4f7b

Farnam Street. (2020). The Man in the Arena: Citizenship in a Republic. Retrieved from https://fs.blog/2009/12/the-man-in-the-arena/

Go Strengths. (2020). What is Grit? Retrieved from gostrengths.com/what-is-grit/

Stevenson, J., Orr, E. (2017). We Interviewed 57 Female CEO's to Find Out How More Women Can Get to the Top. Retrieved from https://hbr.org/2017/11/we-interviewed-57-female-ceos-to-find-out-how-more-women-can-get-to-the-top

Stevenson, J., Orr, E. (2017). We Interviewed 57 Female CEO's to Find Out How More Women Can Get to the Top. Retrieved from https://hbr.org/2017/11/we-interviewed-57-female-ceos-to-find-out-how-more-women-can-get-to-the-top

Hewlett, S. (2014). Executive Presence: The Missing Link between merit and Success. New York, NY: Harper Collins Publisher.

Perlis, M. (2013). 5 Characteristics of Grit—How Many do You Have? Retrieved from https://www.forbes.com/sites/margaret-perlis/2013/10/29/5-characteristics-of-grit-what-it-is-why-you-need-it-and-do-you-have-it/#3620244a4f7b

Perlis, M. (2013). 5 Characteristics of Grit—How Many do You Have? Retrieved from https://www.forbes.com/sites/margaret-perlis/2013/10/29/5-characteristics-of-grit-what-it-is-why-you-need-it-and-do-you-have-it/#3620244a4f7b

Go Strengths. (2020). What is Grit? Retrieved from gostrengths.com/what-is-grit/

Hanford, E. (2012). Angela Duckworth and the Research on 'Grit'. Retrieved from http://americanradioworks.publicradio.org/features/tomorrows-college/grit/angela-duckworth-grit.html

Duckworth, Angela. (2016). Grit: The Power of Passion and Perseverance. New York, NY: Scribner.

Hanford, E. (2012). Angela Duckworth and the Research on 'Grit'. Retrieved from http://americanradioworks.publicradio.org/features/tomorrows-college/grit/angela-duckworth-grit.html

Sadler, B. (2016). Fostering grit in the youth of today. Retrieved from https://www.canr.msu.edu/news/fostering_grit_in_the_youth_of_today

Hunter, C. (2019). Grit: A Key Ingredient for Leadership, With Insight from Executive Andrew Malek. Retrieved from https://www.einnews.com/pr_news/490552299/grit-a-key-ingredient-for-leadership-with-insight-from-executive-andrew-malek

CPSIA information can be obtained
at www.ICGtesting.com
Printed in the USA
FSHW022149281021
85692FS